Family Building

Other Books by John Rosemond

Teen-Proofing

Raising a Nonviolent Child

Because I Said So!

*John Rosemond's Six-Point Plan for
Raising Happy, Healthy Children*

*Parent Power! A Common-Sense Approach
to Parenting in the '90s and Beyond*

Ending the Homework Hassle

Making the "Terrible" Twos Terrific!

To Spank or Not to Spank

A Family of Value

John Rosemond's New Parent Power!

Family Building

The Five Fundamentals of Effective Parenting

John Rosemond

Andrews McMeel Publishing

Kansas City

05 06 07 08 09 RR4 10 9 8 7 6 5 4 3 2 1

ISBN-13: 978-0-7407-5569-9
ISBN-10: 0-7407-5569-2

Library of Congress Cataloging-in-Publication Data
Rosemond, John K., 1947–
    Family building : the five fundamentals of effective parenting / John Rosemond.
        p. cm.
    Includes bibliographical references.
    ISBN 0-7407-5569-2
    1. Parenting. 2. Child rearing. 3. Family. I. Title.
HQ755.8.R663 2005
649'.1—dc22
                                        2005047519

www.andrewsmcmeel.com

Design by Kelly & Company, Lee's Summit, Missouri

ATTENTION: SCHOOLS AND BUSINESSES
Andrews McMeel books are available at quantity discounts with bulk purchase for educational, business, or sales promotional use. For information, please write to: Special Sales Department, Andrews McMeel Publishing, 4520 Main Street, Kansas City, Missouri 64111.

Willie and I dedicate this book to our two children, Eric and Amy, their spouses, Nancy and Marshall, and our six grandchildren—Jack, Patrick, Thomas, Connor, Anna (She Who Will Rule), and Holden.

Contents

Thank you!

To Willie, for your patience and steadfast support.

To Chris Schillig, my editor at Andrews McMeel, for your discipline and steadfast support.

To all the families I come in contact with through my travels as a public speaker and through the World Wide Web, for your input and your willingness to share your ups and downs, and your steadfast support of my mission.

Introduction

Back to the Future

Several years ago, on a flight from Charlotte to Miami, my seat-mate was an older woman who told me she was going to visit several great-grandchildren. We began exchanging snippets about ourselves, and I discovered that she and her husband had seven children, all of whom were doing quite well—no divorces, no addictions, no ne'er-do-wells. They had started out with nothing, she said, and had known a good degree of hardship early on. During World War II, for example, while her husband served two tours of duty in the European theater, she worked in a munitions factory to help the war effort. Her children were taken care of in a government day-care center attached to the factory. In other words, she had been a single, working mother—something the present generation of women seem to think they invented—under the most trying of circumstances. As she talked, it occurred to me that today's parents tend to think child rearing is especially trying even under the most auspicious of circumstances. Yet she was talking very matter-of-factly, as if nothing about her life was that unusual.

"I have to ask," I said. "When you were raising your kids, did you feel, and was it a shared feeling among your female peers, that the raising of children was especially *hard*? Did it leave you emotionally drained and physically exhausted at the end of many a day?"

She looked at me with a somewhat bemused expression and then said, "Why no. It was just something you did."

Just something you did. She wasn't discounting the importance of raising children, not by any means. She was merely saying that she had played a number of roles in her adult life and in each case had given her best to the tasks involved. She had functioned as a wife, sister, daughter, employee, friend, neighbor, and, yes, mother. She had probably performed community service through her church and/or women's groups. In short, she had taken on many duties and responsibilities in the course of her rich life, the raising of children being one of them. Let me phrase that in a slightly different way: the raising of children being *but* one of them.

If outcome is indication, she was a most excellent parent. But she had not let the raising of children *consume* her, as do so many contemporary moms. She had kept it in its proper perspective. She paid more than adequate attention to her children's needs but did not overfocus on them or put them at the center of her life. As a consequence, she was able to go about the duties of motherhood in a relaxed, probably almost casual manner. This is not to be confused with laziness—far from it. She insisted that her children listen and obey, do their chores, display good manners, do their best in school and otherwise, and be helpful toward others. But her insistence was not fraught with tension. It was conveyed firmly but calmly. She probably never yelled at her children. She simply spoke in what was known as "no uncertain terms," and her kids understood that disobedience was not an option.

What a contrast with today's parents, and especially today's mothers! Today it seems taken for granted that child rearing—*parenting,* as it is now called—is, as many parents have expressed it to me, "the hardest thing" they've ever done. How did something that fifty years ago (and beyond) most parents thought was fairly simple and straightforward become so difficult?

"Oh, John," someone might answer. "Don't be naïve! Times have changed!"

That explains nothing, actually. Times have always changed. My grandparents, born in the 1890s, experienced more change in the first thirty years of their lives than did anyone reading this book (think automobiles, airplanes, telephones, and World War I). Yet child rearing did not change. My grandparents raised their children the same way they themselves had been raised. My parents, born around 1920, experienced more change in their lives than anyone raising kids today (consider short skirts, the Great Depression, World War II, and nuclear power). But they raised me according to the same precepts and principles that had guided their parents, and they used pretty much the same methods. No, the fact that "times have changed" explains nothing, because as times changed before the postmodern era (which began, in earnest, around 1960), child rearing did not change. So what caused something that was once simple to become complicated, something that was once relatively easy to become extremely demanding and difficult?

People like me, that's what; people with capital letters after their names—psychologists, social workers, child development specialists, family therapists, and the like. It was the "experts" who coined the term *parenting*, and when American parents began listening to the supposed experts, that child rearing, now "parenting," became "the hardest thing" anyone could take on in adult life. It's people like me—I'm licensed to practice psychology in North Carolina, a license that is recognized as legitimate by all forty-nine other states (although I am a certified heretic in my profession)—who muddied child rearing's once clear waters, obfuscated its simplicity, and downright near killed the common sense of it all.

Once upon a time, when parents needed advice (and they always have), they went to elders in their extended families or communities, most likely neighbors or people they went to church with. Today's parents don't trust elder advice when it comes to "parenting." They trust "experts" like me. Instead of going down the street, ringing a neighbor's doorbell, and asking to come in and talk awhile, they go to a mega-bookstore and buy a book. That's how this book got into your hands, isn't it? When's the last time you called your mom and asked her your child-rearing questions?

Once upon a time, people raised their kids the way they themselves had been raised. Then the so-called experts said that old-fashioned child rearing was bad for children. It scarred their psyches, damaged the holy "inner child," denied children the right to high self-esteem, and caused them to grow up with "issues." The newfangled professional experts said that if children were to have a shot at good mental health—high self-esteem—everything about child rearing had to change. Now child rearing is "parenting," and "parenting" is "the hardest thing . . . ," and never in the history of mankind has a nation of children been so ill-mannered and ill-behaved, not to mention susceptible to problems of every imaginable sort and some yet to be imagined.

It is telling, indeed, that since American parents began to reject traditional parenting and embrace what I call "postmodern psychological parenting," every single indicator of positive mental health in America's kids has been in decline. To cite but one example, today's child is at least three times more likely to commit suicide before age sixteen and at least five times more likely to be diagnosed with severe depression before the same age. Isn't it interesting, for example, that when children were told they had to eat whatever their parents put on their plates because children were starving in Europe, there was no such thing as anorexia nervosa? Beginning in the 1960s, the "experts" told American parents to stop using the sort of discipline used by their own parents, and they did. As a direct consequence, today's parents—one generation down the road from this parenting revolution—have more hassles in the area of discipline than their grandparents even thought possible.

"John," said a woman in Lafayette, Louisiana, several years ago, "I'm absolutely certain that my husband and I have had more problems with two children in four years than my parents had with all ten of us the whole time!"

That is very sad, and I believe that most American parents would probably say something similar. That's even sadder, but it is the inevitable consequence of taking something that wasn't broken and deciding it needed to be fixed. At the behest of the "experts," American parents threw away something that wasn't broken and replaced it with another system that may have looked promising but has not lived up to any of its promises. American parents bought a pig in a poke, and the pig has turned out to be not just worthless but troublesome to the point of being vicious.

The truth is, child rearing is not complicated. Therefore, it is not "hard." There will be difficult moments, of course, and some children, from the get-go, present more of a challenge than others, but if a parent is experiencing the rearing of a child or children as generally difficult— as emotionally, intellectually, and even physically exhausting—then the parent is doing something wrong. If "hard" is the norm, then the parent's attitude is out of whack—she's trying to be her child's friend, for example— or her priorities are out of whack, or both her attitude *and* her priorities are out of whack. She's become her own worst enemy because she doesn't understand the fundamentals of successful parenting, the simple common sense of it all. The following statement is axiomatic: If you undertake a task without understanding the basics, then the task will be hard; understand the basics, and the task will be relatively easy.

The ubiquity of the complaint (or is it a boast?) that "raising a child is the hardest thing I've ever done" is indication that American parents have their priorities seriously out of whack. I've been married for thirty-seven years. I'm happy to report that the single hardest thing I've ever done is stay married that long. By comparison, assisting in the raising of two children was a cakewalk—and they were not, by a long shot, "easy" kids. My own experience, therefore, leads me to conclude that people who complain about how hard it is to raise children are doing something mighty, mighty wrong. If staying married isn't the hardest thing they've ever done (assuming they're still doing it), then they must be slighting their marriages in the course of paying so much attention to their children.

Like any task—geometry, for example—parenting is relatively easy if one understands and masters the basics, the fundamentals.

Reading this book will not only introduce you to those fundamentals but also equip you with the skills essential to mastering them. In the spirit of keeping it simple, I've distilled the fundamentals down to five so you can count 'em on one hand. You might even consider writing one on each finger (and one on your thumb), so as to keep them at your fingertips at all times.

But before we get to the fundamentals, we need to understand what raising a child is all about—the goal. The fundamentals must be aimed at a goal because they are the means to that end. Believe it or not, most of today's parents can't tell you what they're shooting for. I've asked quite a number of parents, "What is your goal?" and most of 'em look at me like I'm speaking Klingon. Or they give me an answer along this line: "I want my child to grow up to be happy."

Happiness isn't a goal. It's the unintended consequence of reaching a goal. That's right, *unintended.* The last group of people who made happiness an end in and of itself were the hippies, and they didn't find happiness. They were some of the most miserable people ever, and I know this to be true because my wife and I tried being hippies for several years in the late 1960s and early 1970s. Believe me, hippies pretended they were happy. They also didn't have any goals, because happiness, as I've already said, isn't a goal. The hippies accomplished nothing because when your ultimate goal is a non-goal, it is impossible to accomplish anything. The only hippies who accomplished anything were those who, like myself, woke up from the bad dream and stopped being hippies. Yes, happiness is the *unintended* outcome of doing things the way they should be done, of living a moral life, of being a good neighbor, of discharging one's responsibilities properly, of being honest in one's dealings with others, of showing compassion for those less fortunate, of doing unto others as you would want them to do unto you, and so on. You want to be happy? Follow the Ten Commandments.

As further proof that real happiness is an *unintended* consequence, take people who say things like "If I only had a new house (job, car, et cetera), I'd be happy." Have you ever noticed that when they get their new houses, their new jobs, their new cars, or whatever it is they claim will make them happy, they still aren't happy? Again, happiness is the unintended consequence of living a right life, not of acquiring the "right" things.

A fellow recently summed it up about as well as I've ever heard it stated. He came up to me during a break in a seminar I was giving in Hilton Head, South Carolina, and said, "John, along the lines of what you've been talking about, my parents weren't thinking in terms of my happiness. They wanted me to be a good person, and they always said that if I was good, I'd be happy too."

His parents probably never read a parenting book, yet they knew, intuitively, that their goal should be to raise a child who was a good, decent human being—a person who did the right thing even when there was no payoff in doing so. Such a person, they knew, would be happy, but raising a happy child was not their goal. The goal was to raise a good kid, one who would do the right thing even when temptation beckoned (which it always does). Happiness was a side effect.

When I was a child, one of the things parents and teachers were fond of saying (along with "because I said so") was "Good citizenship begins in the home." Thinking back on that aphorism, I eventually realized that once upon a time, people weren't even raising *children*. They were raising *adults*. Parents of not so long ago, before Postmodern Psychological Parenting swept the land, had their eyes on the horizon. They weren't simply trying to get through the day, one day at a time. In just about everything they did, they were consciously shooting at the goal of producing a *good* citizen, the sort of person I've tried to describe in the preceding paragraphs.

Today's parents have been brainwashed. They think it's all about something called high self-esteem. I'm going to spend an entire chapter debunking the psychobabble that's built up around this nefarious concept, but for now I'd simply like to emphasize a paradox, one to which I've already alluded: When the goal of raising a child was to produce a *good* citizen, children were a lot happier. If the per capita rates of clinical depression among children then and now are any indication, children were at least five times happier. That should tell you one thing: The "experts" got it all wrong.

We're going to spend the rest of this book trying to get it right.

1

Fundamental Parenting Principle One

*It's About the Family, Not the Children
(Or, First Things First)*

*For this reason, a man will leave his father and mother
and be united to his wife, and they shall become one flesh.*

—Genesis 2:24

Toward the end of the introduction, I said, "The 'experts' got it all wrong." I was, of course, referring to psychologists and other mental health professionals who in the 1960s began to present themselves (with the media's adulatory help) as the Pied Pipers of American Parenting. American parents were persuaded to reject child-rearing principles and a parenting style that had served Western civilization well for thousands of years and embrace a set of child-rearing ideas that had been cut out of a whole different cloth. The family, once parent-centered, became child-centered. Mom and Dad effectively unmarried each other and married their kids. And the American family has been upside down, inside out, and turned around ever since.

Are the "experts" any smarter? Nope. Take Dr. Phil. I first became interested in the Dr. Phil phenomenon when people began telling me, shortly after he burst onto the scene as Oprah's show psychologist, that he and I were a lot alike. I'm naturally curious, so I went to his web site. Several red flags immediately went up. First, the following bit of punditry—offered in the context of "getting right" in relationships: "It's not about what's right and wrong. It's about what works." That sort of statement emanates from a philosophy I reject: pragmatism, which holds, in effect, that the ends justify the means. Pragmatists embrace that which is expedient and convenient, and they believe that morality is a relative construct. It's a notion, says John F. MacArthur in *The Power of Integrity*, "that inevitably leads to compromise of conscience and convictions."

Here's my response to Dr. Phil's pragmatic pronouncement: No, it most definitely is *not* a matter of what works; it's a matter of what's right and what's wrong. I, for one, would rather do what is right, even if it doesn't "work." I am comforted in knowing that I am not alone in this. The fact is, contrary to what Dr. Phil apparently believes, there is no such thing as morally neutral behavior. That's a postmodern myth that appeals to people who want permission to be morally lax, permission to believe that the ends justify the means.

Dr. Phil is obviously a spokesperson for those who do not recognize the reality of Universal Truth, those who want to believe, as does Dr. Phil's mentor, Oprah, that truth is self-defined and can be discovered through introspection, by getting down inside oneself and discovering one's "inner child" or "inner Buddha." This point of view is reflected in Oprah's frequent use of the expression "*your* truth." It's a worldview that justifies self-centeredness, self-righteousness, and the denial of immutable standards of right and wrong. So, right away I know that Dr. Phil and I are not on the same page.

The second thing that strikes me about Dr. Phil is the supposed range of his expertise. He can help you improve your self-image, get your marriage (or any other relationship you're in) back on track, get your sex life right, your business relationships right, and he can help you lose weight. In other words, Dr. Phil claims that he is capable of being All Things to All People, a postmodern Enlightened One who holds the keys to nearly every aspect of personal satisfaction. Needless to say, I'm more than a tad bit skeptical of people who make such sweeping claims. Unfortunately, as reflected in his high ratings, there are lots of people who are taken in by this hype.

The third thing that jumped out at me was Dr. Phil's humble contention that, by following his advice, people can bring about sweeping positive change in their lives in five days! Fancy that! A promise of that inflated sort appeals to a person with a short attention span and, therefore, an affinity for instant gratification. Personal and professional experience convinces me that while a person can have what feels like a dramatic, life-changing experience as the result of participating in an intense three- to five-day group therapy or "encounter" experience (see Dr. Phil's Get Real Challenge), these "conversions" don't stick. Three months if not three weeks later, the person who emerged from such an experience flush with a commitment to change the way he or she lives, the person who was babbling hyperactively about the new insights he or she had gained, is back to square one—blaming others, acting like a victim, and inflicting his or her narcissistic self-righteousness upon any and all within earshot. Everything about Dr. Phil screams New Age, pragmatism, secular humanism, moral relativism, postmodernism.

Next, I sampled some of his shows, and I have continued to do so over the years. There is something that disturbs me greatly about bringing people on television and encouraging them—as happened on a recent *Dr. Phil*—to confess personal bombshells like adultery. This is sensationalism disguised as therapy, and it makes *Dr. Phil* seem to be nothing more than a more sophisticated version of *The Jerry Springer Show*. But then perhaps it's not a matter of whether any of this is right or wrong; it's a matter of the ratings, and they are good.

I was very intrigued by Dr. Phil's book *Family First* because it dealt with my subject matter. I bought it, I read it, and it did not surprise me. It was more or less what I expected: a politically and psychologically correct rehashing of the same old stuff American parents have been hearing from mainstream parenting "experts" for thirty-plus years. For example, whereas the book's title suggests it's about creating a strong family, the contents are all about raising children, about paying attention to and having wonderful relationships with one's children. A significant portion of the book is devoted to suggestions concerning discipline. It's all about the kids, in other words. Not once does Dr. Phil say that truly effective child rearing depends on a strong marriage, that the bond between husband and wife must be *stronger* than the bond between parent and child. In fact, the only conclusion that can reasonably be drawn is that Dr. Phil believes a strong family is all about a strong parent-child relationship.

In some cases, Dr. Phil gives what I think is downright bad advice. For example, in his section on blended families, he says that stepparents should pretty much step back when it comes to the discipline of their stepchildren, leaving it to the biological parents. This is a recipe for disaster! When children are involved, the primary reason second marriages have a higher failure rate than do first marriages is that biological parents will *not* vest stepparents with full disciplinary authority. Usually, this involves mothers refusing to let stepfathers discipline, relegating the stepfather to the sidelines in the "family." He becomes an onlooker, a peripheral figure whose only significance is that he enables a mother and her child or children to live in better digs than would otherwise be the case, assists Mom with logistical matters (getting the kids to after-school activities on time), and helps her relieve her sexual tensions. This does not describe a family, folks, but it does describe the dysfunction found in too many so-called blended families and stepfamilies.

In talking with people whose spouses brought children into the marriage, I hear the same refrain over and over again: "I'm not allowed to discipline his/her kids. Supposedly, according to some book he/she read, this would be confusing to them. I'm not their *real* mother/father, so if I disciplined them, they would resent me and would probably take out their resentment on my spouse—their *real* parent—because they would feel betrayed by him/her. At least, this is what I'm supposed to believe. They have no reason to respect me, therefore. I've concluded that my role consists of making their lives easier. At the same time, I'm supposed to understand that the kids walk all over me because they have 'divorce issues.' It's the only way they can express their anger. Discipline from me, I'm told, would only create more psychological problems for them. Under the circumstances, what am I supposed to do?"

Dr. Phil's advice on this one issue reveals that he has little appreciation for what *family* really means. A family is a social unit that is organized, ideally, around a strong marriage. I say *ideally* because a family organized around a single parent can be viable, can function well, but is definitely not the ideal, and I'm sure that even most single parents would agree. The strength of the two-parent family depends upon the strength of the marriage. The strength of the marriage, furthermore, is critical to the children's sense of security. Whether both members of the marriage are biological or adoptive parents or one is a stepparent is irrelevant. I repeat: The strength of a family depends on the strength of the marriage that created the family.

Yes, a single mother and her children constitute a family, but when she remarries, she is not just adding a man to her already existing family; she and her new husband are creating a brand-new family. The old one no longer exists. This is a new family, and it needs new rules and understandings, one of which should be that Stepdad must have full disciplinary authority over the kids. Another is that the kids must obey Stepdad. If that understanding and that rule are not in place on Day One, the family is going to have trouble. When she remarries, Mom has got to gently "divorce" her kids, and she needs to inform them beforehand that this is going to happen lest they have illusions that after her remarriage Mom is still going to be "theirs" in the ownership sense of the term.

No, I'm not "like" Dr. Phil. We both speak our minds, but that's where any similarity begins and ends.

Teaching Marriage and the Family 101

At this point, I want to go back to something I said earlier: The relationship between husband and wife needs to be *stronger* than either of their relationships with any of the children or the children as a group.

In an interview, a journalist asked me: "When they become adults, what will be the biggest problem facing today's kids?"

I answered: "That most of them are not developing a functional sense of what is truly meant by *marriage* and, therefore, *family*."

Today's all-too-typical child is prevented from learning what marriage is all about by well-intentioned parents who rarely act from within the roles of husband and wife; rather, they act almost exclusively from within the roles of mother and father. This is the new American ideal, based on the nefarious modern notion that the more attention you pay to, the more involved you are with, and the more you do for your child, the better parent you are.

I am a member of the last generation of American children to grow up in families where the marriage, warts and all, occupied center stage. The mother was a house*wife*, not a stay-at-home *mom* in perpetual orbit around her kids. Even if she worked outside the home, as mine did, the fifties mother did not arrive home from work bearing a load of guilt which she attempted to discharge by putting her children at the center of her attention and bustling around them through the evening. The father, when he came home from work, had no intention of romping with his children all evening, "rebonding" with them. He came home looking forward to spending a quiet evening with his wife, his intended partner for life. After dinner, Mom and Dad retired to the living room for coffee and conversation, and the kids found things of their own to do, like homework, which they did on their own as well. They did not slink off into the Land of Unwanted Children. There were exceptions to this general rule, of course, but there are two living generations (mine and my parents') who remember that once upon a time in America, the husband-wife relationship was stronger than the parent-child relationship, as it should be.

"Come on now, John," someone is saying. "You don't actually mean *stronger than*. You mean *as strong as*."

No, I mean *stronger than*. Unlike today's mom, the mom of the 1950s and before was not married to her child; she was married to her husband. And unlike today's dad, the dad of bygone days was a husband first and a father second. He was most definitely not his child's best buddy (the new ideal in American fatherhood). Under no other circumstances can children learn what marriage truly means and involves; and that learning is far more important than being an honors student or a star athlete—infinitely more important, in fact.

If you want more proof of why the husband-wife relationship should trump that of parent and child, consider this proposition: Nothing makes a child feel more *insecure* than the fear that his parents' relationship is shaky, that it might come undone at any moment. It follows that nothing makes a child feel more *secure* than knowing his parents' relationship, while not perfect, is strong enough to endure any hardship, any disagreement.

The primacy of the husband-wife relationship gives a child full permission to begin preparing for his emancipation. The fact that he is not essential to his parents' well-being—that their well-being is contained within their marriage—gives him full, unfettered permission to venture out into a life of his own. A child's leaving home should be cause for celebration, exciting and full of promise for all concerned. When the parent-child relationship is foremost, however, emancipation is difficult for all concerned. Sometimes, the child is able to leave physically but not emotionally. An example of this is the husband or wife who puts more stock in his or her parents' opinions than in his or her spouse's. At other times, emancipation takes the form of a painful "divorce," from which it is difficult for any of the parties involved to ever fully recover.

Today, we have "empty nest syndrome" and "boomerang kids." The former is the consequence of being so wrapped up in one's children that one's life loses much of its meaning when they leave, not to mention it becoming painfully obvious that the marriage lost meaning a long time ago, shortly after the birth of the first child. Not surprisingly, the risk of divorce is very high for people who have recently emancipated their youngest child. The term *boomerang kid* is new because more than thirty years ago there weren't enough kids of that sort to require a name.

The greatest gift one can give a child upon his emancipation is not the keys to a new car or condominium but the security of knowing that, in the truest sense, he can always come home again—not to live, mind you, but to visit. I have spoken to many emancipated young adults who tell me that the greatest pain in their lives involves the turmoil they go through in deciding how to split up visit time between Mom's house and Dad's.

Sometimes our own children tell Willie and me how lucky they are that we are still together and that they know we always will be. It's actually a slip of the tongue, because they both know luck has nothing to do with it. It is a matter of keeping relationships in their natural order and not letting things that are of no ultimate importance take priority over things that are.

Speaking of Things That Are of No Ultimate Importance . . .

I told a recent audience, "I can virtually guarantee that by making one simple decision, you can reduce parenting stress by more than half, create a more relaxed, harmonious family environment, and provide your children with more carefree childhoods. Raise your hand if that sounds good to you." It looked to me as if everyone had a hand up.

"Okay, here's the deal," I continued. "Tell each of your children he or she can participate in only one after-school activity—including a church youth group—at a time. If you have more than one child, tell them that their combined activities cannot take up more than two weekday afternoons and Saturday morning, nor can any activity interfere with dinner, which will be at home nearly every evening, with everyone present. Furthermore, tell them that there'll be no activities during the summer months. The summer is for the family. Do I have any takers?"

No one raised a hand. There was total silence. Four hundred and fifty pairs of eyes stared at me as if I'd just proposed they jump off a cliff. Come to think of it, to the contemporary American parent, taking one's children out of after-school activities is probably akin to committing parenting suicide. How can they demonstrate their commitment to their children without this public display?

I've yet to hear a good counterargument to my proposal. One riposte is to the effect that children enjoy these activities. "How," a parent asks, "can I tell my child he can't do something he enjoys?" Answer: The parent says, "You can't do everything you want to do." It's really that simple. Do you get to do everything you want to do? No? Then why should your children? And aren't the needs of the family unit more important than what an individual child might want or like? Besides, when your children are no longer children, no one is going to make sure they get to do whatever they like to do. And the family would benefit greatly, everyone agrees, from parents who are relaxed instead of in almost constant "hurry up, we gotta go" mode.

This may come as a shocking revelation, but it's true: Children do not *need* these after-school activities and programs. The overwhelming majority of them are superfluous add-ons to an already good life. In 99 percent of cases, the activities any given child is enrolled in today are going to be irrelevant to anything he or she is doing at age thirty. Furthermore, if he or she was *not* enrolled in these activities, that child would probably be doing the same thing at age thirty that he or she would have done otherwise, and just as successfully. I said as much in front of a small group once, and an audience member rejoined, "But what if Tiger Woods's parents hadn't started him in golf so early?"

I answered, "Then maybe Tiger would have grown up to become a virologist and discover a cure for AIDS."

Let's face facts: Tiger Woods is not making a great and wonderful contribution to the betterment of mankind. It's a sad comment on our collectively misplaced values that the average American regards Tiger—a nice fellow presumably—as the modern equivalent of a hero. What obstacle in life has Tiger overcome? What has been his epic struggle? None and none. Therefore, Tiger doesn't qualify as a hero, not by a long shot.

Someone might well ask, "But what if my child has a lot of innate talent for, say, music, and I never let her develop that talent?"

Remember, I didn't say take your kids out of *all* after-school programs; rather, let each of them choose one. If your child has a lot of musical talent, and she values music as much as you value her talent, she'll chose a musical program as her one activity. If she doesn't choose what you'd choose for her, then your child will take her talents (there's no such thing as having simply *one* talent, you know) and put them into some other area. By the time she's forty, there's little doubt she'll be as successful in whatever path she's chosen as she would have been if she'd walked the path you chose for her. No, that's not true. The truth is that a child will always be more successful at something he chooses for himself than something his parents choose for him.

Here's another guarantee: The more relaxed the family unit, the fewer discipline problems you'll have to deal with. A good number of discipline problems experienced by today's parents are nothing more than products of stress. The child under stress is likely to behave in stressful ways, and parents under stress are likely to overreact to and otherwise mishandle misbehavior. Stress produces impatience, which leads to impulsive, ineffective responses to disciplinary issues. The combination is deadly and spirals downward quickly. The less stress you're under, the more relaxed (and thoughtful) will be your approach to discipline, and the more relaxed your approach, the more effective it is. So by taking your children out of after-school activities, you'll have better behaved children! And you'll be a better behaved parent! With more discretionary time, your children will be better able to focus on homework and need less "help" (a.k.a. enabling) from you. They'll even have time for chores. Think of it: children who are actually "earning their keep" and acquiring a solid service ethic at the same time!

One more guarantee: Less focus on children, combined with a more relaxed family atmosphere and definitely more relaxed parents, translates to a stronger marriage. No reasonable person would argue that being relaxed lends itself to better communication and intimacy, and there is nothing as important to the health of a family as the health of the marriage. I'm not saying that single-parent families can't be healthy. I'm simply asserting an undeniable truth: If you're married with children, then the well-being of your family depends fundamentally on a marriage that is strong and fit. Furthermore, the statistics are incontrovertible: Children from intact families do far better along every dimension than children of divorce.

So, how about it? What a wonderful world it would be if the typical American family's number one after-school pastime was "Let's just relax and enjoy our happy home."

Someone recently asked me, "When they were kids, did your children participate in anything except family activities?"

As a matter of fact, family *was* their number one after-school activity. Eric, now thirty-six, played pee-wee football for part of one season, until the coach decided to make him starting quarterback. Eric promptly asked us if he could quit, explaining, "Everyone's out to get the quarterback, and I'm scared I'll get hurt." We let him quit, but he had to inform the coach himself. He then played soccer for one season but didn't like it enough to do it again. When we asked him why he didn't want to play any longer, he told us that the coaches and parents took winning too seriously. He wasn't including us in that evaluation because we rarely even came to his games. We couldn't help but agree with his astute analysis, so he quit, again informing the coach himself. That is the total history of Eric and after-school activities, except for the fact that, as a teenager, he participated in a Christian youth group called Young Life.

When our daughter, Amy, now thirty-two, was nine years old, she announced that she wanted piano lessons. After two months of lessons and the recommendation of her teacher, we bought her a piano with the understanding that, because of the investment required, she had to take piano lessons as long as she lived in our home. But, we added, she didn't have to practice unless she wanted to. Practice was between her and her teacher. Amy took her last piano lesson during her last semester in high school. She landed roles in a handful of community theater productions during her preteen and early teen years, and she also participated in Young Life.

During our active child-rearing years, my wife, Willie, and I witnessed what happened when children's after-school activities dominated a family's discretionary time. The parents never seemed to have time for themselves or their marriages; they frequently complained of exhaustion and stress (as if the exhaustion and stress were not the result of choices they had made); and everyone in the family seemed to be in a constant state of hurry.

Willie and I decided that our children were going to look back on a family life that had been relaxed and relatively carefree. We were going to put family first in the Rosemond household. We were marriage-centered, not child-centered. Eric and Amy did chores (*most* of the housework, in fact, from ages nine and six on, until they left for college), did their own homework, and developed hobbies with which to occupy their spare time. We watched very little television. In fact, for a significant portion of our child-rearing years, we didn't even have a television. The things we did together were activities that produce good childhood memories—picnics, hiking, camping, white-water rafting, traveling, and the like. And we ate dinner together, at our own table, nearly every evening.

Eric is now happily married with three children. He is a corporate jet pilot. He spends his time off with his family. He and Nancy and their three very active, well-behaved boys live in our hometown of Gastonia, North Carolina. There's nothing more important to Eric than his marriage and the family he and Nancy are creating. He quit pee-wee football and he quit soccer, but Eric is anything but a quitter, as evidenced by the fact that he paid for most of his flight training himself and was flying jets at age twenty-four—very young for a nonmilitary-trained individual.

Amy is a happily married homemaker and mother of three. She and Marshall have settled in Dallas, Texas. Although she's well-educated, intelligent, and has very marketable skills, she'd rather be at home building a family than doing anything else. Her family eats almost all of their dinners at home as well, and they are not "hurry up, we gotta go" affairs.

The ultimate joy of parenthood is watching a child grow into an adult with good, solid, traditional values—in other words, a good citizen. As Grandma said, "Good citizenship begins in the home." Not on the soccer field but in the home. Not in a day-care center but in the home, the "classroom of the family."

Dr. Laura and I Aren't Sitting in a Tree

On the matter of priorities within a family, I don't agree with Dr. Laura Schlessinger either. I knew right away I didn't agree with her when I heard her introduce herself on her syndicated radio talk show as "my child's mother." Never mind that she and her husband came first, that their child is a *consequence* of their "firstness." Never mind that marriage is intended to survive the children's (in this case, child's) leaving home. Dr. Laura is a mom before she is a wife.

Since we have different views about family priorities, Dr. Laura and I probably are going to disagree about a lot of things, such as her stand on day care. To summarize it: Day care is bad. No child should be in day care. There are no circumstances that might warrant an exception to this rule. That's it, end of discussion. Dr. Laura has said it; therefore, it is incontestable.

Schlessinger thinks anyone who has a child and then puts him or her in a day-care center is self-centered, placing material values ahead of the needs of the child. That's no doubt true of some people, but others who put their children in day care are doing so in order to secure better futures for the kids, to make sure they can pay for orthodontics and send them to college. That's realism, not materialism, nor does it qualify as self-centered pragmatism.

As for Schlessinger's charge that the parents in question are self-centered, many working parents overcompensate for the time they spend away from their children by putting them at the center of attention in the evenings and on weekends. In so doing, they unwittingly create child-centered families that are not ultimately in the best interests of either their children or themselves. In such a setting, it's the child who is likely to become self-centered. Working parents do not necessarily put their kids low on the list of priorities. Many, in fact, tend to err in the opposite direction. Their priorities are confused, but they are not necessarily self-centered.

The matter of children and day care is far more complex than Schlessinger makes it out to be. She is right to raise the issue but wrong to portray her opinion as the final word on the subject. Instead of her being a "helping" professional, Schlessinger's unbending dogmatism on this subject is decidedly unhelpful.

There are times when day care is absolutely necessary. In fact, day care has always been essential, but it hasn't always been called that. It has always been necessary for mothers to do things that meant separation from their children for periods of time that warranted entrusting the kids to another adult. The difference is that, up until relatively recently, when a mother had to leave her kids in someone else's care, that person was almost always a close relative who lived within walking distance. Unfortunately, that very accommodating set of circumstances is no longer available to many women. Today, women who need to leave their kids in someone else's care almost always have to leave them with someone they hire (an in-home caretaker) or an institution to which they pay "tuition" (i.e., a day-care center).

I hardly think that all of the parents who drop their kids at day-care centers across the USA do so out of necessity, and if necessity is not the case, then I am against putting a child in a day-care center for any significant period of time. Nonetheless, I do believe there are circumstances that justify the decision, circumstances that constitute necessity. Personal experience leads to my opinion in this regard. My mother was a single parent for most of the first seven years of my life, and during that time she worked and went to college. Since she had no close relative with whom to leave me, I spent many a day at Three Little Pigs Nursery School. My mom had no choice. It was that, be tossed out into the street, go to the poorhouse, or give me up for adoption. I can't tell you how happy I am that she put me in Three Little Pigs Nursery School.

Dr. Laura is right about one thing, though: Day care—no matter the quality—is risky business.

Is Day Care Really Caring?

We live in postmodern times characterized by rampant anti-intellectualism. It matters not, for example, that objective evidence says a certain statement is true; what matters is whether or not people *like* the statement. More to the point, a fact is not a fact if it offends some special interest group.

I was reminded of this by the general reaction to Professor Jay Belsky's finding that children who spend lots of time in day care during their preschool years are three times more likely to be aggressive than children whose moms care for them at home. Belsky's credentials are impeccable (Professor of Psychology, University of London), and his ongoing research into the effects of day care, while controversial, has always made sense. Day care and home care are qualitatively different; therefore, the outcomes are not going to be the same. Furthermore, no sensible person would argue that a paid day-care worker can provide a better developmental environment than a loving mother. Therefore, with a nod to the relatively rare exception, home care is better than day care. In fact, I've never met a day-care director who felt otherwise.

In this case, common sense should tell us that Belsky is correct. A child who spends some five out of seven days per week in day care from early infancy, competing with lots of other kids for toys, space, and attention, is likely to be more aggressive than a child who spends his or her days at home. But to many people, Belsky's data and common sense don't matter. They are outraged that he would have the temerity to publish.

Mike Barnicle, a columnist for the *New York Daily News*, said Belsky was "demonizing" parents who put their kids in day care. Echoing the sentiments of anti-intellectuals across the USA, Barnicle called Belsky a "pinhead intellectual" and had the gall to say he should not even have conducted his study if it wasn't going to yield results that made working parents feel good.

The anti-intellectualism over Belsky's data wasn't limited to the naysayers, though. I was asked by CNN to participate by phone in a discussion of Belsky's results, and it was less a discussion than a shouting match. One of the participants, an Atlanta radio talk show host, said lots of moms call her show to testify that deciding to stay home with their kids was the best decision they ever made. So? What does the fact that some moms would rather be at home than at the office have to do with

Belsky's findings? A fair number of moms have told me just the opposite: They think their kids are better off in day care. My point is that personal testimonies neither validate nor invalidate Belsky's research. They are personal. Belsky is doing social science, not personal science. His results, as he would admit, do not necessarily predict individual outcomes.

Nonetheless, there's still that matter of common sense. Common sense says mom care is generally better than employee care. Common sense says day care is going to breed more aggressive behavior than home care. The fact is, Belsky's findings line up fairly well with common sense. Furthermore, his data are supported by other findings. For example, as the number of young children in full-time day care has increased, so have the incidence and severity of childhood behavior problems. That doesn't mean day care is causing all those problems, but it's undoubtedly playing a role.

About ten years ago, in my syndicated weekly newspaper column, I said that it was time we stopped pretending that, for a preschool child, being taken care of in the best day-care center in the world is no different from being taken care of at home by a loving, responsible parent. Needless to say, I argued that home was better than day care. In fact, good research (including Belsky's) supporting my position was just beginning to come out, and since then, there's been a lot more of the same. Kids who, from an early age, spend significant time in day-care centers are more likely to have serious behavior problems (e.g., aggressive tendencies), shorter attention spans, more health problems, and later academic difficulties than are children who are taken care of at home by a responsible parent.

The *Des Moines Register,* one of the newspapers that carried my column, decided to go to war with me concerning this issue. Over the next few months, a *Register* columnist, a guest columnist, and one of the editors (in an unsigned editorial) all attacked me for my position. In one of these rants, I was accused of "setting the cause of women's rights back twenty-five years." Can you imagine that? Little old me, acting alone, in a mere fifteen column inches, was able to do something so earthshaking as to set the clock of women's rights back twenty-five years!

The fight isn't over, folks. In fact, it's just begun, and the fight is for the American family. Karl Marx himself said that the traditional, autonomous, intact family constituted the most formidable obstacle to the establishment of socialist utopian dreams. In my estimation, when both parents decide to go to work outside the home and put children in day care, this weakens the family. It puts the children in an environment that is second best. It exposes parents and children to unnecessarily heightened stress. The only justification for making the decision to have both parents work outside the home is money, and that, it turns out, is not much justification at all.

Studies show that most second incomes are almost completely consumed by an increase in the family's tax rate (the second income nearly always throws the family into a higher tax bracket), child care costs, increased medical costs, increased clothing costs, increased transportation costs, and increased food costs (two-parent-working families eat in restaurants far more often than do one-parent-working families). About the only thing that goes down is the electricity bill. But banks will generally loan a lot more money to two working parents than to one working and one nonworking parent. So not only does the two-parent working family end up with higher monthly bills but it also ends up deeper in debt. More debt equals more stress, more arguments between husband and wife, less intimacy, poorer communication in general, insecure children, and so on. Any way you cut it, it is undeniable that having a parent in the home, taking care of the needs of the family, is the best of all possible worlds. A family simply works better when there's a parent in the home, doing what he or she can during the day to ensure that the home environment is as stress-free and relaxed as possible.

Real Moms Rule!

I was leaving a recent speaking engagement when I felt a tap on my right shoulder. I turned and found myself face-to-face with a diminutive woman, twenty years or so my senior.

"Thank you, John," she said. "Now I get it."

I was mystified. "I'm sorry, ma'am. What is it you get?"

She proceeded to tell me that her thirty-five-year-old daughter, a self-proclaimed "radical feminist," was raising her four-year-old grandson out of wedlock.

"She didn't marry the father, John," she said, with a hint of sadness in her voice. "In fact, she says she'll never marry. She thinks marriage is just a means by which men dominate women, or something silly of the sort. I don't know where she came up with such things. Not from me, I can tell you."

She went on to say that her daughter occupied the highest management position ever held by a woman in the corporation for which she works. She runs an entire department that consists mostly of men. She's on her way up in the company, for sure.

"And, John, after listening to you for the last ninety minutes, I get it. Now I understand how it is that my daughter can tell men what to do all day long and then go home and take orders from my four-year-old grandson!"

Yes, today's women are certainly a paradox. They have taken important strides forward politically, professionally, economically, and educationally, and yet, when they become mothers, they indenture themselves to their children in perpetuity. Their children often talk to them as if they were lower than slaves, and they do nothing about it. Their children demand things of them, and they comply. Their children yell at them, and they cringe. There are even epidemic numbers of American children who hit, kick, and spit on their mothers, who do nothing but try to talk to these out-of-control brats about what's supposedly bothering them.

What's going on here? The problem is that today's mothers are trying to clear what I call the "mother bar"—a contemporary standard of good mothering which endorses the idea that the best mother is the busiest mother, the most attentive mother, the mother who provides the most for her children, fixes it whenever they get upset, drops what she's doing to be at their beck and call, helps them nightly with their homework, and makes sure each of their brain cells is properly stimulated from the womb on.

Contrast all of this with the typical mother of fifty years ago. That very formidable woman intimidated her children; they did not intimidate her. She was not their servant; rather she was there to teach them to stand on their own two feet. If one of her children talked back, he regretted it, and if he got carried away and hit her, well, the first time would have been the last.

Yesterday's mom had no problem at all defining her autonomy to her children. She had no reservations about saying, "I don't have time for you right now, so run along," "If you can't find something to do, I'll find something *for* you to do," "Leave me alone, I'm busy," and "No, I won't do that for you, because you can do it for yourself."

Today's mothers don't feel they have permission to say those things to their children, and if they do slip up and say something as self-esteem-damaging as "I'll give you to the count of five to disappear and stay disappeared for the rest of the afternoon," they feel guilty. And then they apologize, saying things like "I'm sorry. I didn't mean it. I'm just having a bad day," and they start acting like servants again.

Once her child was capable of using the toilet on her own (twenty-four months) and knew to stay out of the street, yesterday's mom tried, on a daily basis, to have as little to do with her as possible. To the contemporary ear, that may sound dreadful, but check it out with someone of my generation. We will tell you it wasn't bad at all. In fact, it was downright wonderful to have a mom who wasn't bustling about in your life all the time, who supervised you well but didn't want you indoors on nice days. These were moms who not only left their children alone (sufficiently supervised) but also wanted their children to leave them alone. Yet with the inevitable exceptions, we Boomers have fond memories of moms who loved us as powerfully as they disciplined us.

The outcome was children who learned at relatively early ages to stand on their own two feet: to fix their own snacks, to fight their own battles, to do their own homework, to entertain themselves, to study for tests on their own, to paddle their own canoes, to stew in their own juices, to lie in the beds they had made, and to accept responsibility for their own mistakes and failures. Mom won, child won, child's teacher won, community won, culture won. Not a bad deal, if you ask me.

By contrast, today's mom fights her child's battles, stews in his juices, paddles her child's canoe, lies in the beds he makes, et cetera. Which brings us back to the thirty-five-year-old radical feminist mom in the preceding anecdote: Ironically, and tragically, she is not teaching her son to respect females, to recognize the legitimacy of and respond appropriately to female authority. Instead, she's teaching him that women are for serving men. She's training her son to be the very man she loathes!

It's not her fault, really. Radical Feminist Hear Me Roar Mom is only submitting to cultural pressure and myth. The cultural pressure involves the nefarious notion that the mom who is the most "involved" with her child, does the most for her child, and pays the most attention to her child is the Best Mom of Them All. This pressure is enforced by other moms and prevents mothers from claiming their authority over their children. So the children, being so inclined in the first place, claim authority over them. This pressure has reduced all too many of today's mothers to being enablers, rescuers, and fixers for their children. The cultural myth involves the notion that the mom who works outside the home, and is therefore not around to enable, rescue, and fix during the day, must come home from work, put her child at the center of her attention, and dance as fast as she can around him from the moment she walks through the door until he consents to go to bed. That describes the standard guilt-discharging ritual, does it not?

Thus, the mother-child relationship in America is all too often inverted. To demonstrate the point, I conduct a little sentence completion experiment in front of audiences around the USA. It goes like this:

I say, "Fifty years ago, the American child was afraid of his mother; today . . ."

And without a moment of thought, the audience responds, ". . . the mother is afraid of her child." I've conducted this exercise at least one hundred times, and *every single* audience has responded as described. Most of the people who chime in on cue are women. The men sitting next to them know the answer, but they are not going to admit it. They're smarter than their wives give them credit for.

Isn't this a sad commentary on American parenting?

"But I don't want my child to be afraid of me, John!" a mother once rejoined.

"And that's why you're having discipline problems with your child," I replied.

"How did you know I was having discipline problems with her?"

"Because," I said, "she's not afraid of you."

Like kids of my generation, I was afraid of my mother. Don't misunderstand. I did not lose control of my bladder when she entered the room. I didn't shrink back when she reached out to hug me. She was affectionate, accessible, and loving. I never doubted that she loved me with all her heart. Still, I was afraid of her. The only way I can explain this is to say that she always acted like she was in control. Furthermore, she never hesitated to tell me I *wasn't* running the show. She acted like she knew what she was doing, and she acted like she knew what I was going to do.

"It's time for you to pick up these toys," she would say, and I would pick up my toys.

"We're leaving now," she would inform me, extending her hand, and I would take her hand and leave with her.

"Today, I'm going to teach you how to wash a floor," she said one day when I was four, and I followed her lead and learned to wash a floor.

The *fear* of which I speak was the same sort of fear that is referred to in the Bible's Book of Proverbs, where we are told that it is good for His children to *fear* the Lord. This fear, it says, is the beginning of many good things, including knowledge and wisdom. It does not say that the Lord is pleased when one of His children fears him. It does not say that it pumps up His ego when He is feared. It says that the benefits of this fear accrue to us, His kids. My fear of my mother—an awesome, inarticulate respect for the tremendous power she represented in my life—benefited me. It was the beginning of good behavior and respect for women.

It is so sad that many of today's children are being denied the same benefits by moms who have knuckled under to cultural pressure and myth. Like I said, it's not their fault; nonetheless, they are the *only* people who can fix this culturewide problem. In my mind, fixing this problem is more important to the future than getting doctorates and becoming CEOs of major companies.

Okay, So What About Dads?

There are predictable differences in the ways mothers versus fathers relate to and interact with their children. These differences have to do with biology, psychology, cultural expectations, and practical considerations. For example, in all human cultures mothers have been primary caretakers to children during infancy and toddlerhood. This arrangement has been dictated by necessity as well as the fact that females are generally more nurturing than males.

During the first two years of a child's life, the typical father functions as a "parenting aide," serving as the mother's assistant. He assists her in her nearly full-time child-care ministry and relieves her when she needs a break. (Despite the increased attention given to "fathering" in the last decade, the exceptions to this rule are still few and far between and, I suspect, always will be.)

Of necessity, the typical mother is "enmeshed" with her child during infancy and early toddlerhood. Between her child's second and third birthdays, however, she begins to step away from her child, expecting him to act more for himself, to stand on his own two feet. In the process, the mother slowly but surely transforms herself from a caretaker to an authority figure, from a servant to a teacher of social values. As the mother's ministry of constant service draws to a close, having fulfilled its purpose, the marriage is restored (or should be) to center stage in the family. At this point, the father's role becomes increasingly crucial to his child's success in a number of areas. Studies have shown, for example, that male and female preschoolers whose fathers are actively involved in their upbringing tend to be more outgoing, adaptable, and accepting of challenge.

Several years ago, in response to a newspaper column I had written on the importance of fathers, a single mom admonished me for suggesting that single moms can't do as good a job as two married parents. She wrote, "In reality, you don't need a father at home to have appropriate male role models."

That's true, as far as it goes. It has become politically incorrect to say so, but all child-rearing situations are *not* equal. As David Blankenhorn, president of the Institute for American Values and author of *Fatherless America* has meticulously documented, children reared by single moms simply do not do as well on any measure as children reared in an intact family unit. There are individual exceptions to this finding, of course, but the general rule is well-established. In other words, while it is true that males other than fathers can be appropriate male role models, it is wrong to assume that the role of fathers is not unique.

A father's mere *presence* in his children's lives is not enough, however. The operative term is *actively involved*. I'm speaking of a dad who is a vigorously interested participant in the child-rearing process—not a perpetual parenting aide or a guy who sits in front of the television demanding that everyone be quiet. Children privileged with involved fathers tend to be more self-confident, outgoing, and independent. In addition, they possess generally better social skills, exhibit fewer behavior problems, and do better in school than children whose fathers are either absent or on the sidelines.

Unfortunately, close to half of the children born in the 1990s will spend a significant part of their growing years in a father-absent home. Adding to this growing crisis are those divorced fathers who rarely if ever see their children. As child psychologist Urie Bronfenbrenner pointed out in a 1989 UNESCO address, such children are at significantly higher risk for all manner of behavioral and educational problems.

Recently there has been a tendency to demonize the traditional father, characterizing him as a remote, forbidding authoritarian who controlled his children through fear. This certainly doesn't help efforts to give fathers the credit they are due and restore dignity to fatherhood, nor is it generally true. Alexis de Tocqueville, author of *Democracy in America,* described the nineteenth-century American dad as stern but forgiving, strong but flexible. He listened to his children and humored them, educated them as well as demanded their obedience. As Blankenhorn points out, the typical American dad has always been a hardworking paragon of traditional masculine virtues. In short, he is a good role model for his children, especially his boys.

As the teen years approach, the role of fathers seems to become even more crucial to good adjustment. Researchers consistently find that teens with active fathers are less prone to have problems with sex, drugs, or alcohol and, even when socioeconomic factors are controlled, are more likely to go to college, enter successful marriages, and eventually become good parents themselves.

Today it's impossible to have a discussion about teens without the subject of sex coming up. Indeed, the early teen years are defined by insecurities concerning identity and sexuality. Fathers can contribute much toward helping their children successfully resolve these issues. The young teenage girl, for example, is beginning to look to males for attention and verification of her femininity. A father's caring attention and affection will go a long way toward satisfying a daughter's need for male approval, thus reducing the likelihood that she will act out her insecurities through sexual experimentation.

Similarly, a male who enters his adolescent years without a dad will often fill the vacuum by creating and then acting out a fantasy of what being a man is all about. This fantasy often includes the idea that "manliness" is a matter of sexual conquest and/or aggressiveness. Again, an actively involved dad can help a son develop a more balanced view of manhood, thus mitigating the notion that sex and physical dominance are crucial to self-worth.

If you're a dad, here are some ways you can become a more powerful influence in your child's life:

1. Find at least one activity you and your child can enjoy doing together—hiking, biking, tennis, coin collecting, or just walking. Then make the time to do it on a regular basis.

2. Help your child develop a hobby, and if your child shows an interest in a specific extracurricular activity, be supportive.

3. As your child grows, work to become less of a disciplinarian and more of a mentor. During the teen years, remember how important it is that the two of you make the transition from parent-child to adult-adult. Take it from a dad whose children are both adults and have

children of their own, the teen years set long-standing precedents in the father-child relationship. Make sure they're positive ones.

4. Communicate! Always encourage your child to use you as a sounding board to talk about any personal or social issue. Make the time to talk with your teen child about the future. In all these ways, you can help your son or daughter clarify and develop a permanent set of sound, positive values.

5. Love your child's mother with all your heart. Show your child not only what being a good dad is all about but also what being a good husband means.

6. Last but by no means least, remember that a child is never too old to be told, "I love you."

The *Family* Has No Bed

The mother asked, "John, why is something that humans did for thousands of years suddenly not good for humans to do?"

She was referring to children sleeping with their parents. Called the "family bed" and recommended by Dr. William Sears and other advocates of "attachment parenting," this co-sleeping arrangement is fast becoming one of the standards of good parenting. If you allow your child to sleep with you, the implication is that you are a more devoted parent than one who insists upon separate beds.

"First," I answered, "the fact that something took place during a less civilized age is hardly proof that it is good. Take cannibalism, for example, or sacrificing maidens to the volcano god. Second, sleeping together was done for the purpose of protection when the level of threat during the night was considerably higher than it is for a modern family. Third, as soon as people could afford a second bedroom, the children moved into it."

"But what's the problem?" she asked.

"Boundaries," I replied. "Or the lack thereof."

I thought of a fellow psychologist who told me about a family he was seeing because of problems involving the seven-year-old daughter, an only child. The girl's second-grade teacher complained that she was both disruptive and disobedient, that she did not finish work, and that when reprimanded she consistently denied having done anything wrong. The parents had tried everything, or so they claimed. For her misbehavior at school, the girl had suffered the loss of privileges, been confined to her room, and been spanked, once. Her parents had also tried giving her various rewards when she behaved reasonably well in school. Nothing had worked. In fact, the child seemed to take perverse pleasure in being immune to punishments, and giving rewards seemed to make matters worse.

The parents claimed that they had no problems with the child. My friend was puzzled. Finally, during a meeting with the parents, he told them he was at a dead end. He hadn't a clue as to what the problem was or how to solve it. At this point, the father let slip that the child did not sleep in her own bed. She slept with the mother. The father slept in another bed, in another room, so he could be rested for work. One revelation led rapidly to another. It turned out that the child's "obedience" was a result of the fact that the parents never asked anything of her. The parents—Mom, mostly—waited on her hand and foot. No instructions from parents equaled no resistance from child. School was the only place where rules and expectations applied, and the child was letting it be known that no one was qualified to be her boss.

This brings me back to boundaries. They are essential to establishing and conveying authority. A boss who fraternizes with those over whom he or she has theoretical authority cannot effectively exercise that authority. A boundary between the boss and the bossed causes the latter to "look up" to the former. When no such boundary exists, neither will respect.

As is the case in all "family bed" arrangements, this little girl had become a member of the wedding. As a consequence, she had no real respect for her parents; they existed to do things for her, period. Since children's respect for other authority figures begins with respect for their parents, she did not respect her teacher either. Unlike the parents, however, the teacher made demands of this child, which she rejected out of hand. Therefore, although she gave her parents "no problems," she was a major problem in class—a candidate for diagnosis. Not surprisingly, the teacher had recommended that the parents talk to my friend about medicating the child for "oppositional defiant disorder."

Today's parents seem to think that any behavior problem can be solved by using the right disciplinary method. This sets them up to believe that if nothing has worked, their children must have "disorders" of one sort or another. The fact is, effective discipline depends on the preexistence of a certain context, the central feature of which is a boundary between parent and child. That context is lacking when children sleep with their parents.

I'm a real stickler when it comes to boundaries between marriage (or single parent) and child. The nature of the first two years of a child's life is incompatible with such a "barrier," of course, but it should slowly but surely be erected between a child's second and third birthdays. By then a child should not even be allowed in his or her parents' bedroom without first standing outside the door, knocking, and asking to come in. A three-year-old can be taught to do this and expected to remember it. By no means does this boundary reduce the level of affection between parent and child; quite the contrary, it makes affectionate moments much more meaningful. Under these circumstances, I don't have a problem with children occasionally being allowed to come into their parents' beds in the morning, perhaps thirty minutes before everyone rises, for some "snuggle time." And it should go without saying that if a young child requires constant supervision during the most critical period of an illness, it's perfectly all right for the child to sleep with the parents or for a parent to sleep with the child.

Questions?

Q: *My husband and I have a five-year-old daughter and a two-year-old son. Our son is currently in a very clingy phase. Three months ago he had a bad episode of separation anxiety when we changed his sleeping situation. Since then, he's been very Mommy-oriented. He wants me to do everything for him and screams and fights if Daddy tries to do even the smallest thing. During the day, however, he's perfectly fine with his regular sitter. In two weeks I have to go away on business for a few days. Is there anything I can do between now and then to make my being away easier for my son or prepare him for it? I've seen a lot of gimmicky things but didn't know if any of this stuff would work.*

A: My non-gimmicky advice, strange and antipsychological as it may sound, is for you simply to disappear. Long good-byes, an attempt on your part to explain where you're going and how long you're going to be gone, will do nothing but create a soap opera and set the stage for a very difficult separation for both you and your son. He will understand only that you are anxious, and you are leaving, and he's not going along. The inevitable consequence: WAAAAAAAAAAAAAAAAAAAAAAAAH!

Several months ago our daughter-in-law brought our two-year-old grandson, Thomas, to visit with us for a couple of days while she went to a wedding. Grandma Willie told me that Thomas was very "clingy" and "attached to Mom" and would certainly have difficulty separating from Nancy at the point of exchange—the airport. Knowing Nancy, I doubted that, but having learned many invaluable lessons in the course of thirty-seven years of marriage, I said nothing.

I met Nancy and Thomas when they got off the plane. As we walked to the car, where Grandma was waiting, I told Nancy this needed to be quick. She agreed. At the car, she buckled Thomas into his car seat, kissed him, and closed the door. We drove away. It took Thomas about five minutes to realize Mommy wasn't in the car, at which point his face started scrunching up and he got the sniffles. Grandma and I just started talking to him about all the wonderful things we were going to do, and he stopped. Two days later, Nancy arrived to retrieve a perfectly content two-year-old.

By the way, you and your husband have absolutely got to stop letting a toddler decide which parent does things for him. How does a twenty-pound two-year-old not allow his father to do things for him? He screams? So what? He struggles? So what? He acts like he's having the toddler equivalent of a panic attack? So what? Dad should simply go right ahead and do what he came to do. He should pay no attention to the screaming or the panic, and you shouldn't either.

"Yes, Daddy's gonna change you. Oh, that's all right. There, there. Everything's all right, but you can scream if you want to. That's just fine. Daddy loves you; yes, I do."

You and your husband will eventually pay a heavy price if you do not get control of this relationship now. Not tomorrow but now. Today.

Q: *Help! I'm at my wits' end. I am the mother of two boys: six months and thirty-two months old. The difficulty is with the latter. This well-mannered, easygoing, very loving child is having trouble at Mother's Morning Out. This is his second year. Last year he cried every day that I dropped him off but would stop within ten minutes. This year, instead of my walking him in, we use the car pool line (so I don't have to get his brother out of his car seat). When the supervising teacher tries to get him out of the car, he cries, falls to the floorboard, and struggles. This morning he actually growled at the teacher as she tried to unbuckle him. Now I'm getting reports that he has become defiant and disrespectful during school. Yesterday he began throwing things when the teacher reprimanded him for something. She thinks he's insecure because there's a second child in the family, but he doesn't act that way at home. She's also thinking of doing a special reward system for him, which I think is a bad idea. Do you have any suggestions?*

A: First, I tend to agree that this behavior has nothing to do with his younger brother's arrival. This problem started before his brother was born and has simply escalated. Second, I agree that a special reward system is a bad idea. When a child behaves badly, punishment is the answer. Unfortunately, preschools cannot receive certain accreditations if they punish bad behavior. I'm convinced that's one reason why research is now finding that children in day care are more aggressive and disobedient than children who are cared for at home.

Having said all that, the fact that this program is optional overrides all other considerations. When a two-year-old gets into a snit of this sort over attending an optional program and the resistant behavior is spiraling downward, I recommend simply taking him out. It's not worth the battle, and besides, this is a battle you may not be able to win. Let several weeks go by, and then find another MMO program or a smaller, cooperative playgroup. A change of venue may make all the difference.

Q: *How do you get a child out of your bed? Six months ago, I allowed our seven-year-old son and only child to sleep with me a few nights while my husband was on a business trip. Then, when my husband got home, our son begged to sleep with the two of us for a couple of nights. We thought this was fairly innocent, but then he began crying if we tried to make him sleep in his own bed. We compromised by letting him go to bed and leave his television on until he fell asleep, but that keeps him awake until all hours and causes him difficulty waking up in the morning. If we try to get him to turn it off, however, he becomes very upset and—you guessed it—wants to sleep with us. We feel like we've created a monster and don't know how to uncreate it. Please help.*

A: The problem is not so much that your son wants to sleep with you, or that he wants to watch his personal idiot box until the wee hours, but that you and your husband cannot bring yourselves to make decisions that upset him. Yes, you made a mistake letting him come into your bed, and you made a mistake letting him watch television past his bedtime. Actually, you made a mistake when you put a television in his room, but that's another matter. You should know by now that if you give your son an inch, he will want a mile. After all, you've lived with him for more than seven years. But the biggest mistake you've been making for most of those seven years is backing away from decisions that upset him. In effect, you've never forced him to give up being a toddler and begin accepting the Prime Reality Principle: What one wants and what one needs are rarely one and the same. Or, as the Rolling Stone Mick Jagger so eloquently put it, "You can't always get what you want, but if you try sometimes you just might find, you get what you need."

That your son cries when you refuse him the comforts of the marital bed is insignificant, trivial. A child does not know what is in his best interest. The proof of this is the fact that children often become upset when parents make good decisions (e.g., "No, you can't have a BB gun"), and children often jump for joy when parents make bad decisions (e.g., "Yes, I'll buy you a BB gun"). The problem is that, like many parents, you view your child's crying as a psychological event. You think you must fix (correct, eliminate, alter) whatever it is that caused him to cry. This is an example of what I term "psychological thinking," the inexorable consequence of which is paralysis of parental decision making and authority.

A marriage is composed of two people, not three, and a child should not think otherwise. For that simple reason, your son needs to sleep in his own bed, whether he wants to or not. At his bedtime, he needs to go to sleep, not watch television, whether (in either case) he wants to or not. The solution to your problem is for the two of you to straighten your backbones and tell your son in no uncertain terms that when it is time for him to go to bed, he will go to his own bed, and he will not watch television, and he can cry about it for as long as it takes for him to come to grips with it.

This is an example of "reality therapy," and nothing cures behavior problems faster than a healthy dose of reality.

Q: *When my husband and I realized we were guilty of having created a child-centered home, we began cracking down on our very spoiled five-year-old and centering our marriage. After three months, things are going well with one exception. Our son enjoys playing with his ten-month-old brother, but three recent times the baby has started crying, and when I check, big brother has a guilty look on his face. So far, the baby has suffered a scratch under one eye and a red mark on his face where a ball hit him. The most recent incident involved big brother getting too rough and almost making the baby vomit. When big brother is banished to his room for these incidents, he is obviously more upset about being punished than about hurting his brother. His lack of remorse bothers us. As a result, we've put baby brother off-limits for a time. Are we expecting too much?*

A: When a five-year-old boy and a ten-month-old boy interact on a daily basis, the younger one is bound to experience occasional pain. This is the inevitable consequence of having two boys, and you will go slowly insane if you try to prevent this from happening. For the next three to four years, until the physical disparity begins to level out, the younger one will experience more play-related insult than the older one. This isn't necessarily bad, it's just the way it is. Furthermore, the fact that big brother even wants to play with a ten-month-old is a good sign, an early indication of a growing relationship. Count your lucky stars that all indications do not point to early resentment, which might be the case if your firstborn was truly as spoiled as you seem to believe.

I think you may be trying to rectify overnight what took five years to create—your family's child-centeredness. Your impatience is causing you to overreact to a situation that by itself is normal. You're also misinterpreting big brother's reaction to being punished for hurting his sibling. You think he lacks remorse, but I think he's justifiably upset at being punished for something he didn't intend to do.

For example, if I'm trying to stay within the speed limit but I fail to see a "Reduce Speed Ahead" sign and I'm ticketed for speeding, I'm not going to be remorseful. I'm going to be upset (inwardly) about the ticket. After all, it was not my intention to speed. By contrast, if I'm intentionally speeding, trying to shave time off a trip, and I'm pulled over, I'm going to accept the ticket, apologize to the officer, and kick myself in the seat of the pants. I have a strong feeling that your older son is being "ticketed" for unintentionally exceeding his younger brother's "speed limit." Under the circumstances, I'd fully expect him to be more upset than remorseful. He's being punished for being, at worst, clumsy.

When incidents of this sort happen, you should take the opportunity to help big brother understand the baby's limits. For example: "I know you want to teach your brother to play catch, but you can't teach a baby to catch by throwing things at him." Then help him learn ways of playing that won't involve risk of pain to the baby, as in "Roll the ball instead of throwing it." You also need to praise him for his attempts to be such a good big brother, however clumsy they may be at times.

Where correcting your family's child-centeredness is concerned, I recommend that you slow down. It's obvious to me that you didn't create as much of a problem as you think you did. Nothing cures a child of being the recipient of too much attention like a new addition to the family.

Q: *My husband and I have a four-year-old boy and an eight-year-old girl. They both whine, cry when they do not get their way, and seem to think no doesn't mean no. In addition, there is lots of sibling rivalry and hassle when it comes to doing what they are told. Because of the demands of our jobs, my husband and I end up doing a lot of tag team parenting, especially when it comes to getting the kids to their after-school programs, feeding them, and seeing that they do their homework. I feel like all we do is scream and yell. I realize this is a tall order, but can you give us some useful suggestions?*

A: You are describing what I call the "frantic family syndrome," the result of emotional resources that are stretched to the max by an overload of outside commitments. It's fairly clear that you and your husband spend most of your time dashing from one obligation to another, somewhat like the plate spinners on the old *Ed Sullivan Show* would dash from one spinning plate to another. As a consequence, you are a family in name only. I'll wager that you rarely sit down to a peaceful, unhurried dinner together, that the last time you went on a family picnic or took a leisurely stroll through a zoo was too long ago to remember clearly, and that by the time the kids get to bed, you're too exhausted to be husband and wife.

An adult or adults and children who are bound by biological or legal ties can claim the title of family, but to actually *be* a family in the true sense of the term requires a commitment to spending a good amount of time in the pursuit of nothing more than being together, enjoying one another's company. (Sitting in the same room staring at a television set doesn't count.)

Yes, I do have some useful suggestions. First, I have to believe that if one of you quit his or her job, the overall level of stress in your family would come down considerably. Studies have shown that most second incomes do nothing but increase family expenditures and push the family into a higher tax bracket while creating the illusion that the family is enjoying a higher standard of living. The end result is a significant increase in the family's debt load, which makes "necessary" a second income that was not necessary to begin with. If you don't see how you can do that given the debt you've already accumulated, I recommend seeing a financial counselor. In the final analysis, you may have to make a choice between ever-diminishing financial stress and ever-increasing family chaos. The situation will continue to deteriorate if you try to maintain the status quo.

Second, I recommend taking the kids out of most of their after-school activities, or at the very least not replacing one when it expires. In the future, limit after-school activities to one per child per season (except in summer, which should be reserved solely for family activities), with the caveat that no activity can interfere with your ability to sit down together every evening to a relaxed family supper.

I have to believe that the discipline problems you're having with your children will begin to "fix" themselves as your family gains a sense of equilibrium. In any case, you aren't going to be able to discipline the kids effectively until you have restored balance and discipline to the family unit.

Q: *I have two toddlers, twenty and thirty-two months, both boys. Not including thirty minutes of reading and snuggling before bed, how much time each day should I spend involved in activities with them? Also, does it matter how they play? They chase each other around the house a lot, roughhouse, and sometimes ride their riding toys, but they hardly ever play with developmental toys like blocks and puzzles. Is there some way I can stimulate interest in these things?*

A: Regarding how much time you spend in activities with your children, keep in mind that the most important thing parents can do with young children is read to them, which you are already doing. The notion that parents need to get down on the floor and play with toddlers a certain amount of time each day is very modern; i.e., without substance. The fact is, if you feel like getting down on the floor and making a block castle with one of your children, do it. But, if you don't feel like it, then don't. Your children should not learn that you are an on-call antidote for boredom—a playmate. Don't try to fill some Play with the Kids Quota, and when you do play with them, don't conduct "activities." Just play. Have fun. When you've had enough, simply excuse yourself and go do your own thing. In the long run, it is best that they learn to play by themselves. If you feel the need to be involved with them several times a day, then read to them two or three times a day for thirty minutes per session. In addition to developing their imaginations, reading will also calm them down for a while—a benefit to you, I assume.

At this age, a child's play is not very organized, nor should someone take pains to organize it or turn it into a specific "learning experience."

The play of a toddler is spontaneous, active (for the most part), and generally not goal-directed. In short, the running, chasing, and jumping that your boys are doing is very toddlerlike, and in their own boisterous way, they're learning a lot. Another way of bringing some peace into your life is to mandate several periods a day during which the children are separated and must play quietly for, say, fifteen minutes. Use a timer to define the period of quiet. When they are able to handle fifteen minutes, extend it to twenty, and so on. If you persist at this, you just might get to an hour by the time the older child is three.

As for their toys, I recommend that you remove the toys they aren't playing with. As I've said elsewhere, most of the manufactured toys on the shelves today should remain on the shelves. They're worthless. The packaging and bright colors attract a child's attention, but once the toy is in his or her hands, it might have a "play life" of less than fifteen minutes. The toys they aren't playing with should disappear quietly, one or two at a time, and be replaced with boxes, pots and pans, wooden spoons, and so on. Give the toys to charity.

Once you find five or ten toys that your children will play with, start a toy library. Store the toys in a closet, and let each child have only one or two toys at a time. When he's finished with one, he can turn it in for another one. This will slowly help their play become more focused and organized, not to mention dramatically reduce toy clutter around the house.

Q: *My husband and I are about to take a four-day trip, during which we have planned to leave our eighteen-month-old daughter with my in-laws. Grandma works, but she is planning on taking the time off to be with our daughter during the day. We had arranged for a familiar babysitter, but Grandma will have none of it. She also says that we shouldn't be surprised if when we return, our daughter looks at us as if we are complete strangers. This has caused me to have second thoughts about leaving at all. What's your take on this?*

A: I think you and your husband are right to go on a little trip together. Our son and daughter-in-law left their first child with Willie and me for four days when he was but six weeks old. We have always encouraged them to do this sort of thing, reminding them that their marriage, not their children, came first and that it's in the best interest of their children that it remain first.

I also think you are right about the sitter. Your daughter will do just fine with a familiar person. She may, in fact, do a little crying when Grandma hands her over in the morning, but this has a 99.9 percent chance of passing within minutes of Grandma walking out the door. In situations like this, parents and grandparents should realize that a child's cries are not an indication that the separation itself is going to be difficult. Rather they mean that the *act* of separation is difficult. The child gets over the act most quickly if it is quick.

I also agree with Grandma. If she wants to take time off from her job to stay home with her granddaughter during the day, so be it. She should do exactly what she wants to do, and you should stay out of it. After all, Grandma will feel anxious all day at work. She won't fare nearly as well there as your daughter will at home with a sitter. So why not have two calm, secure people instead of just one? Therefore, Grandma stays home, saving you some money.

I generally agree with Grandma, but I must disagree with her prediction that when you arrive home your daughter may look at you as if she doesn't know who you are. C'mon, Grandma, you ought to know better! Consider that a four-month-old puppy recognizes his master after a week's absence and rebonds almost immediately. I think we can safely assume that an eighteen-month-old intelligent human being will know her parents after a four-day separation. At age six weeks, our grandson Jack went right to his parents when they returned from an extended weekend away. Of course, being my grandson, Jack is hypergifted, but I think it safe to assume your daughter, at eighteen months, is at least on a par with Jack at six weeks.

No, you won't come back to a child who is staring off into space, unresponsive, refusing to eat, making no sounds. She will know you and greet you with as much enthusiasm as an eighteen-month-old can muster. She will not have to have recovered memory therapy because of this at age twenty-five, either.

But by all means, humor Grandma. Don't get into a debate with her over this, because you aren't going to change her mind. Just leave! Go! Have fun!

Q: *My four-year-old daughter cannot go to sleep unless I lie down with her, has rarely slept through the night in her own bed, and all of my attempts to correct this situation have failed. She used to become hysterical if she woke up in the middle of the night to discover I was no longer with her. Now she just comes and crawls into my bed. If I make any attempt to persuade her to go back to her bed, she starts to cry. To be honest, I'm a working single mom, and I just don't have the strength to fight it. She knows what I want her to do, but she also knows I have yet to enforce it. Can you provide me with a workable plan that will not cause her—and therefore me—anguish?*

A: No. There is no such thing as an anguish-free method of turning your daughter into an independent sleeper. But before I tell you what will, let me note that your story is proof that independent sleepers are happier children. Let's face it, you are not describing a happy child; rather, your daughter is a four-year-old basket case, a b+edtime neurotic. She is yet another in a long list of casualties of what's referred to as "family sleeping." And to think there are "experts" (e.g., Dr. William Sears) out there who have made their reputations on recommending this emotionally crippling practice, which puts the marriage in the backseat and the parent-child (usually mother-child) relationship in the driver's seat.

My experience with this problem dates back to the mid-seventies, when the "family bed" movement began gaining momentum. Since then, sleeping with one's child, or letting the child come into the marital bed, has become a symbol of the mother's commitment to the child and his or her best interest.

First, let me assure you that solving this problem now is going to be easier than putting it off until next week or next year. I encourage you to begin your daughter's bedtime rehabilitation this Friday night at the latest. If possible, take Thursday and Friday off work and implement the following solution on Wednesday night. That gives you four nights of "cure" before you have to go back to work. Four nights ought to do it. Second, there is no way of doing this without upsetting your daughter. Just keep in mind that her screams are symptoms of withdrawal, and withdrawal is painful but not harmful. Third, the solution will be more traumatic for all concerned if introduced in stages. It absolutely must be introduced all at once, cold turkey, and once introduced, you must not waver.

Here is the solution: Two days before implementation, tell your daughter that you've spoken with her doctor, and he or she said you can no longer, come the big day, lie down with her at bedtime, nor can she come into your bed in the wee hours. Sorry. Shrug your shoulders. You have to do what her doctor tells you to do. The doctor's the boss. But you've decided that after you put her to bed and leave (do not linger!), she can turn on every light in her room and take her time falling asleep. You'll even give her a sleeping bag and set up a tent for her to sleep in if that's what she wants. Sleeping can be an adventure, but she has to sleep in her room. The doctor said so, and that's that.

Furthermore, the doctor said that when you go to bed, you have to lock your door. She can drag her sleeping bag into the hall outside your door and sleep there, but you cannot open your door until morning.

Again, the key is not to waver. Your daughter is probably going to scream, cry, beg, and make promises to the effect that if you allow her to sleep with you just one more night, she'll never ask to sleep with you again. She will believe her own promises. Don't you.

Keep this in mind: When the transition is over, and it soon will be, you'll see a much happier little girl waking up in the morning.

2

Fundamental Parenting Principle Two

*Where Discipline Is Concerned, It's About
Communication, Not Consequences;
Leadership, Not Relationship*

Simply let your "Yes" be "Yes" and your "No," "No."
—Matthew 5:37

The parents of an unruly four-year-old boy asked me to help them develop an effective discipline plan. I asked what they meant by the word *plan*. They exchanged perplexed looks, then the father answered, "Well, techniques we can use to correct his behavior and cause him to behave."

There is no parenting subject more fraught with misunderstanding than discipline. The biggest, most prevalent misunderstanding concerns the nature of discipline itself. Like the parents I just described, who've read too many parenting books and articles written by people who promote Postmodern Psychological Parenting, most parents mistakenly think that effective discipline is all about choosing the right consequence and applying it properly. In other words, the typical contemporary parent thinks that discipline is a *technology*—that it's all about mastering *techniques* like time-out and taking away of privileges and star charts and the like.

That's not it at all. Discipline does *not* consist primarily of a set of techniques or methods properly used. It is *not* all about the clever manipulation of consequences. It is *not* a matter of knowing when and how to spank or use time-out or when to take what privileges away and for how long. It is *not* about "natural" or "logical" consequences. Rather, effective discipline consists of a point of view, an attitude. From this attitude naturally emanates a certain relaxed, self-assured body language; a certain relaxed, self-assured tone of voice; a certain commanding look; and perhaps most of all, clarity of speech.

Effective discipline is not rules but *rule*. It is the process of turning a child into a disciple, someone who will follow your lead. A child who is disciplined effectively will grow to love both the leader and the leadership. He will obey because he has discovered that his parents discipline him *because* they love him and that he obeys them because he loves and trusts them—in effect, he *consents* to their governance. He will question some of their decisions because he can, but he will not rebel, although he can.

His parents do not try to control him, because they know they cannot. They understand what a woman who raised children fifty years ago meant when she said, "Every child has a mind of his own." Therefore, the parents control only that which they can control—their *relationship* with him. Understanding that their child is likely to confuse need and want, *they,* not he, decide what he needs and what he does not need. Having done so, they provide all of what he *needs*, whether he *wants* any part of it or not, and a small amount of what he *wants*, despite his insistence that he *needs* more. In attempting to control only the relationship, his parents determine

1. What they will and will not do, on a personal level, for him. They decide, for example, what kind of help they will give him with his homework and how much.

2. What they will and will not provide in the way of material things for him. In other words, they decide his standard of living, and it is not necessarily a mirror image of theirs.

3. The rules he is expected to follow in the household—e.g., when he goes to bed, what he eats for dinner, his chores.

4. The extent and nature of his freedoms and privileges.

5. The consequences of his behavior, which they can control to a great degree when he is small and to lesser and lesser degrees as he grows older and obtains more freedoms. This is why it's so very important that the foundations of effective discipline be laid early.

But they do not try to control his behavior. They expect him, from an early age, to exercise good self-control, accepting that at age three good is considerably less good than it is at age twelve. They help him learn to control his own behavior by being models of good self-control. They especially model good self-control when he loses his. They help him learn the process of making good decisions—which consists of weighing options, putting off instant gratification, and doing what is right rather than what simply achieves a certain goal—by demonstrating to him that every decision results in a consequence. They teach him that in order for the consequences of his behavior to improve, his behavior must improve.

There are parents who try to control what they cannot, parents who fail to control what they can, and parents who control only what they can. I'll describe each type in turn.

Parents who try to control what they cannot: These parents think it is possible to control children and/or their behavior. Because they are attempting the impossible, these parents are in almost constant psychic pain from beating their heads against the brick wall of immovable reality. They are, depending on when you peek in on them, frustrated, resentful, angry, enraged, or emotionally spent. Basket cases! Who is the *only* person capable of controlling a child's behavior? Why, the child herself.

Parents who fail to control what they can: These parents fail to control the one thing that can be controlled: the parent-child relationship. These parents allow their children to control the relationship, and consequently, they too are in constant psychic pain. They do not understand why their good intentions, noble generosity, and many sacrifices do not produce children who are appreciative and willing to reciprocate with some co-operation every now and again. After all, they simply want their children to like them! The only thing that distinguishes their emotional reper-toire from that of parents who try to control their children is guilt. Their children are on the road to becoming inveterate narcissists, and narcissists are known for feeding like vampires on other people's guilt.

Parents who control only what they can: These parents control the parent-child relationship; no more, no less. One cannot do this during most of the first two years of life, by the way. A child's complete depen-dency at this age precludes it. But parents can and should begin putting this control into place slowly but surely no later than a child's second birthdays. In so doing, the parents begin to control the child's access to them, define what they will and won't do for the child (i.e., what they insist the child does for himself), and control the consequences of the child's behavior. It is possible to control a large share of consequences when children are small, and a smaller and smaller share as children be-come larger; therefore, it is important for parents to exercise maximum control over consequences when such control is most possible, thus setting functional disciplinary precedents. Parents who establish such precedents are rarely if ever frustrated, angry, resentful, enraged, or guilty. They tend to have relatively carefree relationships with their children. Their chil-dren are relaxed, obedient, self-entertaining, responsible, and best of all, happy.

Another way of describing a proper disciplinary *attitude* is to call it "loving leadership." Unfortunately, over the last forty or so years, the "loving" in old-fashioned loving leadership parenting has been all but replaced by indulging, enabling, and rescuing. Powerful, true love has been replaced by a sentimental, weak love that isn't *true* in the mechanical sense of the term (made straight); rather, it wobbles all over the emotional landscape. Enablers inevitably resent the necessity of enabling; then they feel guilty about their resentment. To assuage their guilt, they enable some more, and so on. Similarly, the "leadership" in old-fashioned loving leadership parenting has been displaced by the ubiquitous desire for a "wonderful" parent-child relationship. Under the circumstances, powerful discipline gives way to discipline that is weak. Like weak love, weak discipline is not *true* either. It wobbles from no to yes and then back to no, from trying to get the proper behavior by manipulating rewards, to manipulating punishment, and so on.

True love strengthens. True love must sometimes say, "No, I won't help you. You can do that on your own," and stand firm in the face of the child's dramatic demand that his delusions of helplessness and incompetence be acknowledged and indulged. Truly loving parents are willing to cause their children frustration and resentment, even to cause their children to hate them. They know their children do not realize what is in their own best interest. They know their children often hate a good decision and rejoice in a bad one. They know that "foolishness is bound in the heart of the child" (Proverbs 22:15) and that only a strong love can exorcise this imprudence. Yes, most of today's parents love their children, but they do not *truly* love them with a love that strengthens.

Equally unfortunate these days are the number of parents who are trying to be their children's friends. The new ideal in American fatherhood has become exactly that: be your child's best buddy. Shame on such fathers! The parent who understands that child rearing is leadership understands that a leader cannot be a friend to someone he leads. Friendship cancels leadership. When young, the child needs a parent who is a leader. When the child is an adult, he or she needs a parent who no longer "parents" but has become a friend. To everything in parenting there is a season. To confuse the season is to confuse the child.

It's All in the Telling

I often ask my audiences, "Discipline involves three words that begin with the letter *c: communication, consequences,* and *consistency;* what do you think is the most critical of the three?"

"Consistency!" the audience will reply, in chorus.

The question never fails to elicit that answer, reflecting the fact that today's parents think disciplining a child is no different from training a laboratory rat to press a bar to obtain food or water. It's an honest misunderstanding. After all, that's what psychologists have led parents to believe. Every psychology student learns about how lab rats are taught various tricks—pressing bars, turning in circles, running mazes—by being rewarded when they do the right thing and either ignored or punished when they do the wrong thing. Psychology professors leave their students with the erroneous impression that it is through the use of this technology, called behavior modification, that one disciplines children properly. If you think about it, the implication is that humans and rats share the same psychology: that underneath our civilized veneers, we are mindless creatures who can be controlled through the simple manipulation of reward and punishment. That seems downright silly. It's too silly, in fact, to be even the slightest bit offensive.

First, human beings possess free will, rats do not. Human beings can and will choose to ignore punitive consequences and keep right on doing bad things. Rats cannot and will not. Second, one does not so much discipline behavior as one disciplines character. Rats have no character to discipline. It's all about a rat's behavior. It's all about a child's character. Discipline the proper character into a child, and the proper behavior will follow.

No, the most important of the *c* words is not *consistency.* Remember that discipline is really leadership; it's the process of turning a child into a *disciple,* someone who will follow the parents' *lead.* What is the most important attribute of a good leader? Is it his or her ability to choose the right consequence when someone misbehaves? No. Then it follows that his or her most important attribute is not the ability to apply consequences consistently. That leaves . . .

Communication.

Right! The most important attribute of an effective leader, whether the context is a corporation, a charitable organization, the military, or a church, is the ability to communicate in a way that motivates people to do what they are supposed to do, to *want* to do what they are supposed to do.

Today's parents frequently complain that their children don't do as they are told. That simply isn't true. With occasional exceptions, a child will do what he or she is *told* most of the time. That's a fact, not a theory. The discrepancy between what is absolutely true about children (they will do what they are told) and what parents report (many children do *not* generally do what they are told) is easily explained by the fact that most contemporary parents do not *tell* their children what to do. They ask. They even ask their children permission to ask, as in capping what they think is an instruction with the silliest and stupidest word in contemporary parenting: "Okay?" In addition to asking, they plead, bargain, cajole, and try to persuade, but they rarely if ever simply *tell*. Examples:

"Billy, don't you think it would be better if we did that some other day?"

"Roberta, Mommy would really rather you sat here, okay?"

"I think it's time you were in bed, Suzette, don't you?"

"Let's begin picking up these toys now, Rodney, okay?"

Note that the parents in these examples are not telling. They are making requests that they hope their children will consider favorably. Communication of this sort is lacking in authority. It is servile, and the master—in these cases, the child—does not obey the servant. There is nothing, absolutely nothing, *wrong* with today's children that would lead us to believe they cannot obey as well as did children fifty years ago, when I was seven. My peers and I were mischievous, for sure, but when given direct instruction by an adult, we obeyed. Why? Because our parents and teachers and other adults *told* us what to do. They didn't beat around the bush; they spoke in *no uncertain terms.* Here's how parents fifty years ago would have delivered the same instructions:

"No, we're not going to do that today, Billy. Some other time perhaps."

"I want you to sit right here, Roberta. No, not there; right *here.*"

"Suzette, it's time for bed. Not tired? Well then, my darling, you can lie in bed and stare at the ceiling all night long."

"I need you to pick up these toys right now, Rodney, and the television is going off until they are picked up and put away." (Click!)

The reason most parents don't talk that way to their kids is that they suffer from DLS, Defective Leadership Syndrome. They apparently do not understand that parenting requires servantship during infancy and early toddlerhood and leadership from that point on. Above all else, good leaders act like they know what they are doing, even when they are unsure. Good leaders never have to yell or demand attention in other, equally dramatic ways because they speak authoritatively, and authoritative speech *commands* attention.

A parent who finds himself or herself *demanding* attention and obedience from a child simply has not yet learned how to *command,* and you command not by delivering consequences consistently but by how you *communicate.* And keep in mind that you communicate not just with words but with your tone of voice, your body language, the expression on your face. There are times, then, when you communicate without saying anything at all. Once again (because I can't say it enough), discipline is leadership, and leadership is *not* a technology; it's an attitude that communicates both unconditional love and dependable, reliable leadership—*true* love and *true* leadership.

I use the term *Alpha Parents* for those who have mastered the verbal and nonverbal language that constitutes this powerful, loving attitude.

They are "Alpha" because they loom large, but not threateningly so, in their children's lives. Their discipline is compelling but not loud or dramatic. Sometimes, as with my mother and most moms of her generation, it consists of nothing more than a certain compelling look. For the parent in possession of the Alpha attitude, *just about any disciplinary technique will work in any situation.* Furthermore, discipline will require relatively little effort. By contrast, for the non–Alpha Parent, no disciplinary technique will work for long, as evidenced by the fact that many of today's parents say, "I tried this or that technique, and it worked for a while, but then it stopped working, so I tried this other technique, and it worked for a while, but then it stopped working, so . . ."

Techniques do not produce a well-behaved child. They are only the means of maintenance once proper behavior has been obtained. Good behavior is produced by parents who speak and act like they know what they are doing, know what they want and don't want, and know that discipline consists mostly of clear, concise communication, not techniques.

"This is your chair" usually results in a child who sits in the designated chair. "Mommy wants you to sit in this chair, sweetheart, okay?" often results in a child who resists sitting in the designated chair. The former is declarative, and the latter is a wish. Children do not grant parent wishes.

Milquetoast Parents

Being a frequent traveler, I spend a good deal of my time in public places, where I make a point of tuning in to exchanges between parents and children. After having listened to exactly 457,832 of these exchanges (at this writing), I am no longer amazed by flagrant disobedience on the part of children. What amazes me is that children obey at all.

I've come to the conclusion that most parents talk to their children using "milquetoast speech." Caspar Milquetoast, from a comic strip created by Harold Webster in 1924, was a shy, retiring character whose name derived from an equally timid food—toast drenched in milk. Caspar rarely came out and said exactly what was on his mind, much less actually *asked* for anything. Instead, he hemmed and hawed and mumbled and otherwise acted the wimp. Like Caspar, today's parents rarely communicate their expectations in direct terms; rather, they beat around the proverbial bush.

Example: Mom wants her daughter, Yurmajesti, to begin getting ready for bed. She asks, "Don't you think it's time you were in bed, Yurmajesti?" No fool, Yurmajesti stomps her foot and bawls, "Oh, c'mon, Mom! It's still early! I want to stay up a little longer." Of course, Mom becomes flustered and sputters something about children needing their sleep and yada yada yada. Two hours later, Yurmajesti finally consents to go to bed. Did Mom think Yurmajesti was going to answer, "By gosh, Mom, you're absolutely right. I didn't notice what time it was. Thanks for being so concerned about my overall welfare"?

Another example: Dad wants his son, Aristokrat, to give him a hand with just one of the many household chores. He asks, in an obsequious tone of voice, "Aristokrat, do you think you can tear yourself away from the Internet for a few minutes and take out the trash for us?" Needless to say, Dad ends up taking out the trash.

Parents employ milquetoast speech whenever they whine, complain, plead, entreat, entice, bribe, and explain themselves so as to persuade their children with reasons. The antithesis is the Alpha Speech employed by effective leaders. Parenting is leadership, so it follows that effective parents use Alpha Speech when communicating rules, instructions, and expectations. It is direct, economical, and generally devoid of explanations, threats, or promises. Let's take a closer look at each of these characteristics:

- *Direct* means coming straight to the point, leaving nothing to the imagination. "Do you think you can turn off the television and give me a hand here?" is not direct. In fact, instructions that take the form of questions are not instructions at all. They are requests, examples of "beating around the bush" speech. Here's direct: "I want you to turn off the television and take out the trash."

- *Economical* means not using twenty words when five will do. Alpha Parents are not necessarily curt, but they do not dress their instructions in flowery language. An Alpha Parent would not say, "I realize you're having a good time, but you're making a lot of noise and I'm trying to read, and I wish you'd stop or maybe go somewhere else, okay?" Instead, he or she would say, "You're making too much noise. I can't concentrate. Take it somewhere else, please." That may not sound as nice as the former version, but the nice version is unlikely to result in compliance whereas the not-so-nice version probably will. When you give an instruction to a child, ask yourself whether you are wishing the child would obey or clearly conveying the understanding that obedience is the only option. Only the latter will yield results.

- *Devoid of explanations, threats, or promises* is fairly self-explanatory, and most parents would have no problem with threats and promises. But why should you not explain yourself to a child? Because when you explain yourself to a child, you are acting as if you are seeking the child's approval, as if you are not *telling* but rather trying to persuade. Leaders seldom explain themselves. Some leaders *never* explain themselves. Politicians explain themselves because they're trying to persuade people to agree with them. Politicians want people's approval. Leaders just state themselves. They are not trying to persuade; they are trying to command. They are not seeking people's approval. It goes without saying that many parents act more like politicians than leaders.

To make this point even more clear, I offer the following list of "Top Ten No-No's When Communicating with Your Child":

1. *Phrasing instructions as if they were questions.* This approach implies choice when no choice actually exists.

> **Wrong:** "How about picking up these toys so we can start getting ready for bed?"
>
> **Right:** "It's almost time for bed. You need to pick up your toys and put them away."

2. *Stating expectations in abstract rather than concrete terms.* Using words like *good, responsible,* and *nice* leaves the parent's actual meaning open to interpretation.

> **Wrong:** "I want you to be good in the store."
>
> **Right:** "While we're in the store, I want you to walk next to me and ask for my permission before you touch anything."

3. *Stringing instructions together.* The mind of a child younger than five has difficulty holding on to more than one instruction at a time. With children older than five but younger than ten, it's best to give no more than two instructions at a time. If it's not convenient to hand out chores in this patient fashion, give the child a list. If he or she can't read yet, use drawings.

> **Wrong:** "Today, I want you to clean your room, take out the garbage, feed the dog, pick up the toys in the den, and help me move these boxes into the attic."
>
> **Right:** "The first thing I want you to do today is clean your room. When you finish, let me know, and I'll tell you what comes next."

4. *Preceding instructions with the word* Let's. This is another passive, nonauthoritative form of communication. When you expect a child to do a chore on his or her own, say so. Don't open the door for resistance by implying that you're willing to pitch in.

Wrong: "Let's set the table, okay?"
Right: "It's time for you to set the table."

5. *Following instructions with reasons or explanations.* Putting the reason last attracts the child's attention to it rather than to the instruction itself. This order makes argument more likely.

Wrong: "It's time to get off the swing so we can go home."
Right: "It's time for us to go home now. Get off the swing and come with me."

6. *Making instructions into sales pitches.*

Wrong: "Hey, Sissy! Guess what? Mom's cooked a really great supper tonight! Let's say good-bye to Sally and go see Mom's surprise!"
Right: "It's time for supper, Sissy. You need to say good-bye to Sally and come inside."

7. *Giving instructions with an open-ended time frame.*

Wrong: "Billy, I need you to mow the lawn sometime today, when you get a chance."
Right: "Billy, I need you to mow the lawn today, and I want you to be finished by the time I get home at six o'clock."

8. *Putting instructions in the form of wishes.* This approach amounts to nothing more than a passive complaint about the child's behavior. Children don't grant wishes, genies do.

Wrong: "I wish you'd stop chewing with your mouth open."
Right: "Please stop chewing with your mouth open."

9. *Conveying instructions as exasperated questions.*

Wrong: "How many times do I have to tell you not to chew with your mouth open?"
Right: "Please stop chewing with your mouth open."

10. *Expressing instructions as threats.* This practice invites resistance because the child will almost certainly want to see if you will actually follow through.

> **Wrong:** "Stop chewing with your mouth open, or I'm going to sew your lips shut and feed you through a straw."
>
> **Right:** "Please stop chewing with your mouth open."

One more time now: Discipline is not primarily a matter of what consequences you use when your child misbehaves. It is primarily a matter of effective communication, which is primarily a matter of giving instructions properly. Proper communication will prevent 90 percent of discipline problems.

Yes, punitive consequences play a part in the overall discipline of a child. But without the right attitude—the Alpha attitude and the speech that goes with it—no punishment will work for long. With the right attitude, any consequence will work just about any old time. Parenting is not rocket science.

Four Powerful Words

Three of our six grandchildren spend a good amount of time at our house. After all, they live only three miles distant. During a recent visit, I refused a request from the oldest grandchild, Jack. "Why not?" he asked, a slight whine to his voice.

"Look at me, Jack," I said. He gave me his full attention. "Have I ever," I asked, in the most pleasant of voices, "answered that question with anything other than 'because I said so'?"

He looked at me for a few seconds before responding, "No."

"Then you know the answer, don't you?"

He shrugged his shoulders. "I guess," he said, and proceeded to go about his business unfazed. The next day Jack and his younger brother

Patrick asked their parents to take them to our house. I offer this as proof of the fact that Alpha Speech does not cause children to resent, fear, or dislike adults. Quite the contrary, it simplifies their lives. They might not like it *at the moment,* but they are quite comfortable with it in the long run. Alpha Speech prevents the arguments that ensue when one speaks like Caspar Milquetoast, and be assured, children don't enjoy arguments with their parents any more than parents enjoy arguments with their children.

Do you speak authoritatively to your children, or are you a Caspar Milquetoast? Check it out. Buy a manual counter and keep it with you on a day when you and your children are together. Click it every time you finish an instruction to your children with "okay?" You'll probably be as amazed as a woman who did exactly that and subsequently e-mailed me her report.

"John," she wrote, "in just one day, with three kids, I counted 52 okays! Worse, even though I knew I had to count each one, I couldn't stop myself!"

Caspar Milquetoast, move over!

Patrick and the Great Spaghetti Incident

Once upon a time, I thought discipline was all about punishment. This wrongheadedness had a lot to do with my graduate training in psychology, especially the behavioral aspect of it. When my pet rat, Mad Dog, did something wrong, I gave him the electric equivalent of a spanking, and he straightened right up. I think the statute of limitations has expired on cruel and unusual treatment of rats; nonetheless, I would appreciate it if no one would tell PETA about my sordid past as a rat trainer. In any case, I have long since realized that discipline is primarily a matter of communication, not punishment.

Now don't get me wrong. There's a time and a place for punishment, and every parent should have a plan so that, when the time comes, he or she acts with forethought rather than impulsively. But discipline—the process of turning a child into a disciple, a little person who will follow your lead—is mostly about telling children the way it is and the way it's going to be. This telling must be clear, it must be done calmly, it must be concrete (in words the child understands), and it should most definitely be concise, to the point. The preceding formula is all but guaranteed to make a child listen and do what he or she has been told, which is in his or her best interest (assuming the teller is a responsible adult).

Two of our grandsons spent a long weekend with me and Willie several years ago. One night I fixed my celebrated spaghetti sauce and cooked a batch of pasta to a perfect al dente. When I presented five-year-old Patrick—the younger of the two—with his meal, he promptly told me he didn't like spaghetti sauce. He said he eats only the noodles, with butter on them. I served everyone else and sat down.

"Patrick," I said, calmly, "that's your supper."

Again he told me he didn't like spaghetti sauce, and I told him that, at our house, we all eat the same meal. No one, ever, gets a different meal. Again, more plaintively, he told me he didn't like spaghetti sauce. I told him that it was not polite to tell someone who had fixed food for you that you don't like it. I added that since God had provided the food for us, it was not polite to God. (Some people would say this is an example of "laying on a guilt trip." I maintain it is the truth and withholding such a truth from a child may cause the child less discomfort immediately but will result in more pain and misfortune eventually.) Patrick looked at his grandmother, hoping to be rescued from a fate worse than castor oil. Willie gave him a "that's the way it is" look, so he looked back at me and gave it one more try.

"But I really don't like spaghetti sauce," he said, very sweetly and sincerely. "I've never eaten it."

"Oh, Patrick," I replied. "I'm not saying you have to eat it. I'm saying that's your supper. You don't have to eat it. But Nommie (Willie) and I are not going to fix you something else. Furthermore, you need to know that we have planned ice cream for dessert, but dessert is only for people who have finished their supper—all of it." (Note: I was not bribing Patrick. I was simply telling him the way it was going to be. A bribe would have been conveyed thusly: "Patrick, if you eat all of your supper, you can have a bowl of ice cream. What do you say!")

Patrick looked at me for a few more seconds, picked up his spoon, and started eating. He ate everything on his plate (and I had not given him an "experimental" helping), then announced, rather proudly, that he liked my spaghetti sauce and would eat it again. And, yes, that he will, since I can cook only about seven dishes.

If you think this is a story about getting a child to eat his supper, you're less than half right. This is a story about teaching a child good table manners, especially when at someone else's house. It's also a story about helping a child understand that we should give thanks for everything we have, even if it's not exactly what we want. Effective discipline, you see, accomplishes something in the short term and in the long term, and it's the long term that truly matters.

When Consequences Are Needed

Over the last thirty or so years, mental health professionals have given American parents the impression that proper use of time-out (a few minutes in a chair following a misbehavior) will put an end to any discipline problem. At one time I was a true believer in time-out. I used it with my two children, Eric and Amy, and recommended it often to parents whom I counseled as a family psychologist. I have since come to the conclusion that *time-out works with children who are already well-behaved.* It does not work with children who have developed behavior problems that are outrageous either in kind or in frequency.

A child who walks the proverbial straight and narrow needs only a nudge when he or she falls off the proper path, and a few minutes in a chair will be nudge enough. But a thousand nudges will not suffice to move an out-of-control child onto a path he or she has never walked. To mix my metaphors, using time-out to deal with "outrageous" misbehavior is like trying to stop a charging elephant with a flyswatter. The fact is, the outrageous requires the equally outrageous.

The problem with today's parents is they are reluctant to employ outrageous consequences—and by this I definitely do *not* mean hurtful or cruel—because professional psychobabblers have intimidated them into believing that outrageous discipline is psychologically harmful. Indeed, Big Consequences cause children great discomfort and inconvenience, which is precisely the idea. Are they psychologically harmful? Not unless you think that improved behavior is bad.

A Big Consequence is one which serves to prove, once and for all, that parents mean business—permanently. Consequences of this sort will stop a certain misbehavior from gaining a foothold in a family—what Grandma meant by "nipping it in the bud." A Big Consequence can also be used to stop a full-blown behavior problem—one that's already beyond "bud" stage—in its tracks. Grandma referred to this as "lowering the boom."

Eric's Big Consequence: Two weeks into the school year, one of Eric's fifth-grade teachers called to tell us he wasn't doing his work in any of his classes. He wasn't disruptive, she said, but he was socializing instead of working. Willie and I sat down with him and told him, in no uncertain terms, "Solve this problem." In fact, we trusted so much in his ability to do so that we weren't going to monitor his homework, call his teachers on a regular basis, or in any other way respond neurotically to this red flag.

"However, Mr. Eric," I said, "if your report card, which comes out in six weeks, says you haven't solved this problem, Mom and I are going to solve it for you. Do you have any questions?"

He said he understood, but then that's what they always say when their backs are against the wall.

Six weeks later, his report card came out. It was awful. Once again Willie and I sat down with him and said, "You didn't solve the problem. Therefore, like we told you, we're going to solve it for you. For the next four weeks, if you're not in school or in church, you'll be in your room. You can come out to use the bathroom, do chores, eat with us, and go places with us as a family. During that time, your bedtime—even if there's no school the next day—will be seven o'clock. That's lights out. In four weeks we're going to request a progress report from your teachers. If one of them indicates that you have not completely solved the problem, we'll do this for another four weeks. Eric, let us remind you, you have seven years left to live with us."

Needless to say, he was thunderstruck. Never in his wildest fantasies did he think we'd do something so, well, Big. Four weeks later, when we requested the progress report, the teachers wrote: "We don't know what you did, but Eric has been a completely different child, a model student!"

From that day forth, any time there was the slightest inkling of a problem brewing in school, all we had to say to Eric was "Do you happen to remember the fifth grade?" The next thing we knew, his problem would be not-so-miraculously solved.

Benson's Big Consequence: Benson was a major behavior problem, both in school and at home. He was disruptive, disrespectful, and disobedient. At conferences with his third-grade teacher, principal, and counselor, it was repeatedly suggested that Benson had attention deficit disorder (ADD). The parents were reassured that ADD is caused by bad genes; therefore, his behavior wasn't their fault. Benson needed medication to help him control his impulses, they were told. His parents resisted this well-intentioned drivel for months. (Note: Contrary to what many parents of ADD children have been told, there is no scientific proof, period, that ADD is inherited or the result of a biochemical imbalance or structural anomalies in the brain.)

"Finally," the mother told me, "we reached the limit of our tolerance for his shenanigans. Benson came home from school one day to discover a padlock on the door to his bedroom, which houses his television, video game unit, sports equipment, slot-car racing system, and so on. We told him he'd be allowed in his room for fifteen minutes in the morning to dress for school and for fifteen minutes in the evening to get ready for bed, which was going to be seven-thirty every night, seven nights a week. His bed was going to be the sofa in the living room. Most comfortable, if you ask me."

Benson was stunned to say the least. When he threatened to report his parents for child abuse, they reminded him that he would be properly fed, properly protected from the elements, and sleep in a bed that was much safer than his own. After all, he could roll out of only one side of the sofa!

"But please!" Benson's parents said. "Tell whomever you like how abused you are."

This austere state of affairs would last a minimum of four weeks, they told him. During this time he would not be allowed to participate in any after-school activity, have friends over, use the phone, watch television, or go anywhere except to accompany his parents. Furthermore, every single incident of misbehavior at school or home would add a week to his "exile," and no amount of good behavior would shorten it.

"It was amazing," his mother continued. "His teacher called us several days later to tell us he'd become a completely different child. She'd never seen so much improvement so quickly. He became a model child at home as well—polite, cooperative, talkative, a general pleasure to be around."

Four weeks later the padlock was removed from Benson's door with assurances that it would be reattached at the first hint of relapse. A year later, Benson was still on the wagon, which should surprise no one.

Stompanella's Big Consequence: Stompanella was five years old when her parents decided they'd had enough of her tantrums. These outbursts occurred whenever they refused her anything or insisted that she perform even the most menial of tasks, such as picking up her playthings. Stompanella's tantrums—screaming at the top of her lungs, falling on the floor, throwing things—had started during the terrible twos, which had been most terrible, indeed. And they'd gotten progressively worse. At first she'd confined her fits to home. As time went on, however, she became less and less concerned about her audience. When her kindergarten teacher called to express concern, Stompanella's parents acted—belatedly, but not too late.

The plan was simple. The first time Stompanella threw a fit on any given day, she'd be sent to the downstairs bathroom—safe, yet distinctly boring—and the door would be closed. When she was back in control of herself, she could emerge. The second time, she'd be sent to the bathroom and stripped of all privileges for the remainder of the day. This meant she could not watch television, go outside, or have a friend over. The third tantrum of the day would result in her spending the rest of the day in her room and going to bed immediately after supper. I call this technique "Three Strikes and You're Out!" and have found it to be very effective with a broad range of behavior problems. Stompanella's parents also informed her that until she was tantrum-free for a month, she'd get no new toys, no new clothes (unless they were absolutely necessary), and no treats, and she'd go to no movies or other special events.

Consistent with the adage, things got worse before they got better (as they often will when parents approach a discipline problem *effectively*), but Stompanella's parents stayed the course. Needless to say, Stompanella spent most of the first two weeks of the plan in her room. Finally, she got it, and just like that, her tantrums ceased. That's right, they just stopped. Every once in a while, her parents would see one begin to boil up inside her, but before the first scream emerged, Stompanella would cut it off. She'd turn and stomp off to her room, her mouth sealed shut, to pout. As far as her parents were concerned, pouting represented light-years of improvement, so they wisely decided not to fight that battle.

In Eric's case, Willie and I nipped a problem in the bud by using a Big Consequence. In both Benson's and Stompanella's cases, their parents lowered the boom, thus putting relatively long-standing problems to rest. In all three cases, Grandma's old-fashioned discipline won over modern psychobabble, proving once again that there's nothing new under the sun.

I sometimes refer to Big Consequences as Memorable Consequences, meaning that they take up permanent residence in a child's memory banks, which is their purpose. In fact, consequences that fail to produce permanent, unpleasant memories are ineffective by definition. That doesn't mean, however, that one experience with a Big Consequence is going to be enough to solve a behavior problem. It might, as with Eric and Benson, but don't count on it, and remember that, in those cases, the consequence lasted for four weeks. Even with a Big Consequence, you will have to prove your resolve, your commitment to solving the problem, to your child. Typically, three applications of a Big Consequence will do the trick, but your child just might be one of those who needs more than three applications before he or she is fully convinced that you mean business.

Being Strict

I receive a fair number of letters and e-mails from people who write to affirm my belief that discipline is best when discipline is strict. Sometimes a parent will approach me at a speaking engagement to announce his or her membership in the Society for Disciplinary Strictness.

"I'm very strict," this person will say, with obvious pride, telling me about the many positive comments she receives from other often amazed people concerning her children's good behavior.

Unfortunately, I've recently discovered that what some people think is strict isn't strict at all. It's exhausting, exasperating, obsessive, and silly, but it isn't strict.

On a number of occasions over the past year or so, I've watched some of these pretenders be "strict" with their children. Here's a composite example of how they corrupt the term:

"Rambo! Give me that!"

(Rambo, age seven, acts oblivious.)

"Rambo! Did you hear me?"

"Yes."

"Well?"

"I'm just playing with it."

"I don't care. Give it to me. It's not a toy."

"But, Mom!"

"No! Give it to me."

"Just let me play with it for a while. Please."

"No! Now!" (Mom holds her hand out, expectantly.)

(Rambo jerks the "toy" back, away from Mom's hand.)

"Rambo! Give me that! Now!"

I think you get the picture. This game may go on for two or three minutes before Mom wins, Rambo succeeds at persuading her to let him play with "it" for a while longer, or Dad intervenes and Rambo immediately hands it over. I don't mean to imply, by the way, that the so-called strict parent is always Mom. It might be Dad. It might be both Mom and Dad.

In a time not so long ago, parents of this sort were known as Nags. Other parents—truly strict ones—rolled their eyes at them. In those days, however, most parents *were* strict. Today, most parents are anything but strict. In addition to Nags, today's parents are Wimps, Bullies, Soul Mates, Playmates, Bedmates, Servants, Absents, and Codependents. There are very few true Stricts.

To illustrate truly strict, I'll return to the same example and give it a new outcome:

"Rambo, please hand that over to me. It isn't a toy."

(Rambo acts oblivious.)

(Mom, without any show or feeling of anger, takes Rambo by the hand, leads him to his bedroom, and says, "You're going to be in here for one hour, young man. Furthermore, I'm calling off your spend-the-night with Billy. You can spend the night at his house some other time."

"Mom! Okay! I'm sorry!"

"That's fine, but your apology doesn't change the fact that you didn't do what I told you to do."

"Mom! It's not fair!"

"Rambo, you're a very smart fella. Smart enough, in fact, to figure out that when I talk to you, I mean business. I'm certainly not going to insult your intelligence by repeating myself. Now, I'll let you know when your hour is up." (Mom walks away.)

And that's that. I think you get the picture, but just in case: Strict is letting a child know that words are not simply exhalations of hot air. Rather they mean something. Strict isn't mean (although children sometimes *think* it is), loud, threatening, or even punitive. In fact, my consistent personal and professional experience is that strict parents, because they convince their children that words mean something, punish less and enjoy their children more.

A parent once told me she felt I placed too much emphasis on the need to be strict and not enough on the need to be relaxed and affectionate with children. She said it was her experience that a relaxed parent disciplines more effectively.

I agree, but there is no incompatibility between being strict and being relaxed. In fact, my personal and professional experience leads me to conclude that *the strictest parents are the most relaxed parents.*

Strict discipline is powerful but not harsh. Strict discipline is consistent but not necessarily predictable or repetitious. For these reasons, strict discipline puts a quick end to a problem, nips it in the proverbial bud. As such, it is in the best interest of both parent and child.

Continuing the Rambo example, let's say Rambo gets the message and begins doing what his parents tell him to do the first time they do the telling. Two weeks later, however, he lapses and is sent to his room for another hour and informed that he isn't going to play in that day's soccer game. He protests, cries, pleads. His parent holds fast. It's another month before Rambo ignores a parental instruction, upon which he is calmly punished, and then it's two months before another infraction, and so on. By being strict, his parents have made a disciplinary molehill out of a potential disciplinary mountain. Rambo is better behaved, and his parents are under less stress. In this fashion, the relationship between Rambo and his parents becomes more spontaneous and genuinely affectionate.

In other words, relaxation is the payoff for being an effective disciplinarian.

Weak Discipline Versus Powerful Discipline

Some time ago a good friend told me his five-year-old, in complete disregard of the rules, rode his bicycle off the cul-de-sac on which they live and was found an hour later on the other side of the neighborhood.

"We were terrified," this fellow said. "All sorts of things went through our minds while we were looking for him."

"So," I asked, "what did you do about it?"

"Oh," he replied, his voice taking on a "you better not mess with the Big Guy" tone, "We took his bike away for a day."

It just came out before I could stop it. "Oooooooh!" I crowed, mockingly.

"What?" my friend said, startled.

"You sure are mean," I replied, with a chuckle.

"Oh, right! What would you have done, Mr. Parenting Expert? Taken his bike away for a month?" he rejoined, sarcastically.

"Oh, at least."

My friend looked at me for a moment, then said, "You're serious, aren't you?"

I was dead serious. Here's my prediction: Having been inconvenienced to no significant degree as a result of breaking the rule on riding his bike, my friend's child will break the rule again. He probably already has. After all, what's the big deal of a day without your bike?

However, if his parents had put the bike up for a month, hung it from a hook in the garage, for example, then this little boy would have paid a great price (relative to his age) for breaking the rule. I would predict he never would have broken the "don't ride your bike off the street" rule again. Not ever.

Most of today's parents are like my friend. When their kids do something wrong, they tap them on the backs of their hands with wet noodles. When it comes to corrective discipline, they do not want to upset their children. Ironically, because they will not upset their children, they themselves end up getting upset and yelling things like "How many times have we told you not to ride your bike off the street? Answer me, young man! How many times?" Then they feel bad for having lost their tempers. Then they apologize, and it's back to square one.

If you want a child who has broken a rule not to do it again, when the violation occurs, levy a punishment that does *not* fit the crime, a punishment that is completely out of proportion to the offense. In that fashion, you will make a lasting impression on the child, and the infraction in question is unlikely to occur again. Ever. I'm not talking about spanking, by the way. I'm talking about what parents of old referred to as "nipping it in the bud."

Outrageous consequences of this sort do not have to be levied often. A handful, or one every so often, will serve as a great preventative of future disciplinary infractions. In the final analysis, parents who employ consequences of the "no bike for a month" sort wind up seldom having to punish. Their children take them seriously, and they obey the rules. But parents who tap with wet noodles wind up having to tap, tap, tap, tap, tap, tap. Then, because their children don't take them seriously and keep breaking the same rules, they yell. Then they feel bad, apologize ("I'm sorry. I've had a bad day. I didn't mean to take it out on you"), and start tapping again.

To tap constantly and be stressed out or to be occasionally outrageous and almost always cool as a cucumber: That sounds like a no-brainer to me.

Weak Love Versus Strong Love

Parents who read parenting books are concerned, conscientious, caring, and committed. They are certainly well-intentioned, but that doesn't mean they are doing the right things.

The parents in question love their children, but not all love is equal. Just as it is possible to discipline wrongly, it is possible to love wrongly. Unfortunately, many well-intentioned parents love their children deeply and wrongly at the same time. Like their discipline, their love is weak rather than strong.

Weak love is indulgent, permissive, appeasing. Parents who love weakly generally expect a lot of themselves and relatively little of their children. They want their children to make good grades in school, for example, but they ensure the good grades by sitting with the children as they do their homework, guiding their every move. In so doing, the parents harm the children more than help them. Weak love is also afraid of making children upset, afraid of hearing them yell, "You don't love me!" or "I hate you!"

Strong love, by contrast, is empowering, *but children may not always like it.* Parents whose love is strong understand that children must learn certain things—the most important lessons of all, perhaps—the hard way, through relatively lonely encounters with adversity, by making mistakes and learning from them. Strong love is there to protect but realizes that adversity per se is not reason enough for protection.

Strong love helps a child stand on her own two feet. Weak love lets the child stand on her parents' feet. Strong love requires that the child lie in the beds he makes. Weak love lies in the child's beds for him. Strong love lets the child stew in his own juices. Weak love stews in the child's juices. Strong love is supportive but requires that the child fight his own battles. Weak love fights the child's battles for him.

Here's a story about strong love: My mother holds a Ph.D. in plant morphology, an esoteric life science. She is brilliant, and her brilliance extends to matters of math. One day when I was in the fifth grade or thereabouts, I came to her complaining about a math assignment that was giving me trouble. She looked at my math book, noted that the concept was still being taught the way she learned it, and handed the book back to me.

"I figured this out when I was your age," she said. "You can too."

"Mom!" I protested. "I've been working on it for almost thirty minutes!"

"Oh," she replied, "you're telling that to the wrong person. I've been working on some problems for five years now and still haven't solved them, but I'll work on them until I do!"

With that, Mom dismissed me with an imperious gesture as if she was the Queen of England. My foolish, eleven-year-old heart hated my mother for that. I remember storming away, saying something like "You don't even care!" In fact, Mom cared enough not always to make every-thing better. On those occasions, she forced me to learn that I was capable of solving my own problems. She already knew that about me. I just needed to learn it about myself. Those were the days when if you did not "get it" in a certain subject area, you had to attend summer school. I did not attend summer school; therefore, I must have solved the math problem in question.

You can't bring out the best in a child by just telling him he's capable. You have to make him discover his capabilities, which requires struggle. As a parent, your job is to support your child's struggles but not struggle for him. Strong love, tough love, you can call it what you will. It's real love.

The Home Is Not a Free Speech Zone

I recently had a funny exchange with a person in the sales division of the company that manufactured my once trustworthy laptop. I called the company to order a replacement part, and in the course of confirming that I am the proper owner, the saleswoman asked, "What is the Center for Traditional Parenting?"

"I write books and give seminars on raising children," I answered.

That made her happy because she was having problems with her sons, ages four and three. They talked back to her. They told her flatly that they weren't going to obey, that she was not their boss, et cetera.

"Now," she explained, "I'm trying to raise them to feel they can always speak freely to me."

"Then you're doing a great job!" I exclaimed.

"I am?" she responded, somewhat puzzled.

"Yes, you are," I said. "They obviously feel they have complete permission to speak freely to you."

"But that's not the kind of free speech I mean," she said. "I want them to obey me, not disrespect me."

"Well, I'm sorry to tell you, but you can't have it both ways."

The conversation took on a sudden businesslike tone and ended shortly thereafter.

Like many of today's parents, this mom is trying to put the cart before the horse. In this case, the cart is a "democratic" parent-child relationship; the horse is a relationship in which the child does what he is told because he is told, and the parent tells, not asks. Put another way, children will not appreciate the fruits of democracy, such as freedom of speech, unless they have not had access to said fruits for a period of time sufficient to properly steep such appreciation. Children who are given freedom prematurely will abuse it. This mom's children are quickly turning into tyrants. How ironic! She gives freedom, and they demand entitlement.

Such is the sorry state of child rearing in America, where postmodern psychobabble, not common sense, holds sway. I told a father recently that the way to assure the trustworthiness of a child during the teen years is to insist upon blind obedience when the child is young and gradually loosen the restraints upon "free thinking" as the child approaches adolescence. This all but ensures that the teenager will impose sufficient restraints upon his or her own speech and behavior.

"Oh," the fellow said, "I don't feel comfortable with that."

I felt like telling him it wasn't about him. It was about his child. And it wasn't a matter of what he did and did not feel "comfortable" doing. It was a matter of his child's best interests. Parenting in America is a fairy tale in which childhood, long imprisoned in the dank Dungeons of Dysfunctionality, is being rescued by legions of caring, compassionate parents who want their children to express themselves freely, which they end up doing to the detriment of all concerned.

"I would never have spoken to my parents the way my children sometimes speak to me," a forty-something mom recently remarked, looking like she was about to cry.

That's not exactly right. She would indeed have spoken to her parents in a disrespectful fashion if they had given her license to do so. But they did not. They did not give her free speech prematurely; therefore, she was not a child-tyrant. She was well-mannered, respectful, and obedient. Thus, when the time came for her to enjoy free speech, she did not abuse the privilege.

Sadly, many of today's children never enjoy free speech. They've always had it, so what is there to enjoy?

Questions?

Q: *Our two-year-old son frequently calls my husband by his first name, Frank. He has addressed me by my first name only a few times. We would prefer that our son address his father as "Daddy." We feel this is more respectful, not to mention that my husband wants to enjoy his "Daddy" rights. So far, we have not corrected our son. We feel that drawing attention to behavior may only make it worse. Instead, when he addresses his father by his proper name, one of us will point at his father and ask him, "Who is that?" His response is always correct: "Daddy!" Nonetheless, he continues to call his daddy by his first name. I understand that my clever son is intrigued by discovering and using our names, but how do I make him understand this is not acceptable?*

A: You obviously don't know how to think like a two-year-old. Let me help you. When your son calls his father by his first name and you point at your husband (or he points at himself), and say, in a dramatic voice, "Who's that?" your son thinks you're making the second move in a game—the name-game equivalent of peekaboo. So he proudly replies, "Daddy!" And you gleefully say, "That's right!" And once again, your son has won the game.

If a two-year-old discovers that he can elicit a dramatic response from someone, he will attempt to repeat the sequence at every possible opportunity. This is not willfulness (although twos can indeed be willful). This is fun! It's a two-year-old's attempt at comedy.

In other words, while this behavior is not "bad," you should correct it. Mommy and Daddy (Mom and Dad) may seem informal, but they are titles. First names are not titles, and it should go without saying that one attaches more respect to a title than to a first name. Therefore, your son (all children) should address you (their parents) as Mommy and Daddy.

To stop what your son is doing, you need to stop engaging in what he interprets as a game and correct him, clearly and firmly. When he addresses his dad by his first name, his dad should say, "I'm not Frank, I'm Daddy. Call me Daddy." For the time being, you should also refer to your husband as Daddy. That should end the game and clear up the confusion.

Q: *My husband, who is a sports fanatic, has taught our two-year-old son to "high-five," which our son does by hauling off and slapping the other person's hand as hard as he can. I think this equates to teaching him to hit, but my husband thinks I'm being silly, even though our son once high-fived another toddler so hard the child cried. This business of teaching children to slap other people's upraised hands seems to be common. I'm beginning to feel like an old fogy. What do you think?*

A: I propose that you and I found the Society of Old Fogies Opposed to Teaching Young Children to High-Five, because I too think this practice is dumb, moderately dangerous, and debasing of a child's respect for adults. Mind you, I have no problem with adults high-fiving one another, although I participate in this uncivilized display of exuberance as little as possible. I don't even have a problem with older children hauling off and slapping one another's open palms. It is, after all, childish.

One of the problems with teaching preschool children to high-five is their general lack of self-restraint, especially when the preschooler in question is male. As you describe, preschool boys tend to rear back and slap the other person's upraised hand as hard as they can. The few times I've been foolish enough to cooperate in this inanity, my hand has suffered no small amount of stinging pain. The last time a proud father goaded me into cooperating in high-fiving his two-year-old ego extension, I flinched at the last second, which caused the toddler to miss and go toppling forward with the inertia of his violence. He crashed into a table and cried. I was not the most popular guy in the room at that moment. As I said, that was the last time. In all honesty, there should not have been a first time.

The pain in the palm aside, high-fiving implies a familiarity that simply should not exist between adult and child, even parent and child. In my old-fashioned estimation, this is a practice that should be reserved for mutually consenting peers, age ten and older. Two older kids high-five? Fine. Two adults high-five? Fine. An adult high-fives with a child? Not fine. To me, this is the physical equivalent of a child calling an adult by his or her first name. Children should be taught to address adults with formal titles—sir, ma'am, miss, et cetera—and shake, not slap, their hands.

This high-fiving business is symptomatic of a strong need on the part of contemporary adults to be approved of by children, to be perceived by them as cool. Personally, I have no such need, and I fail to relate to the insecurity inherent to it. This may have to do with the fact that long ago I accepted that children do not approve of me, especially when they discover I'm the guy who, as one nine-year-old recently put it, "ruins children's lives." Being decidedly unpopular with the denizens of Munchkinland has been rather liberating, actually. I recommend it. Besides, my grandchildren love me, and that's all that counts.

My opinion may carry some weight with your husband; then again, it probably won't. He's a sports fanatic, and yelling "Slap me five!" is an integral part of sports fanatic culture, into which he undoubtedly wants to induct his son at the earliest possible age. A man who actually believes that the outcome of a game is of cosmic significance may see attempts on your part to put an end to the high-fiving as downright subversive, as if not to high-five is not to be truly masculine. Which gives me an idea: You can always threaten your husband that if he does not stop the high-five lessons, you will take the earliest possible opportunity to teach his son the art of flower arranging.

I can see it now: "Nice bouquet, son. Slap me five!"

Q: *I recently heard you speak in Wisconsin and realized that I have not made the transition from servantship to leadership with my two girls, who are six and four. Long past the time I should have taken control of my relationships with them, they still call many of the shots. One of the first things I want to do now is stop being their playmate. At present, I play with each or both of them at least ninety minutes every day, sometimes more. Should I continue to play with them at all, or should I begin to expect them to entertain themselves without me? In either case, how should I make the change?*

A: As I told that Wisconsin audience, our culture no longer supports a woman making the critical transition from servantship to leadership. The "mother bar," as I term it, which women feel they must clear in order to validate that they are good mothers, has written on it messages like "The woman who spends the most time with her children is the best mom," "The woman who does the most for her children is the best mom," and "The woman who most successfully fixes the problem every time her kids get upset is the best mom." Women who subscribe to this propaganda are locked into serving their children. Their children, in turn, take them for granted and do not listen well. Why should they? Servants are not supposed to give instruction, and when they do, well, they deserve to be ignored.

Good for you that you are determined to free yourself from the box of parenting correctness (PC). I applaud you, but I also need to warn you that other mothers may be made uncomfortable by your liberation. You need to know that there are negative social consequences for women who take charge of their children and refuse to play by the PC rules. It is nothing short of ironic that supposedly liberated women remain slaves to their kids and don't like it when one of their gender emancipates herself from this nonsense.

No longer serving as playmate to two children who are perfectly capable of entertaining themselves and each other is an excellent place for you to begin. In that regard, I would strongly recommend that you simply tell your daughters what the new program looks like.

"Girls, hear me clearly. I am no longer going to be your playmate. You are old enough to figure out how to occupy your own time. From now on, I expect you to play by yourselves or with each other. If you ask me to play with you, the answer will be no, and you are invited to find that out for yourselves. I will probably make some exceptions to this, because there are times, quite honestly, when I want to be a child myself, but these occasions will be rare. I love you both! Any questions?"

I strongly recommend that you simply "flip the switch" and never turn it back on again. Do not wean them by reducing your playmate time by five minutes a day. The likelihood is you will never finish the job.

Once the girls have adjusted to this change—and there may be some whining, even crying, for a week or so—identify another area of your prolonged servantship and rectify it. In a few months, your daughters should see you in a completely different light, as a powerful, formidable authority figure.

Repeat the following mantra at least ten times a day, while standing in front of a full-length mirror: "I am Mother, hear me roar!"

Q: *My daughter and first child is age three years, eight months. She is generally well-behaved except for a bad habit she has of screaming and running away from me when we leave stores, the library, et cetera. She seems to be throwing these fits because she doesn't want to go home. She'll pull away from me and run. Several times she has run into the street before I could catch up with her. I have spanked her or sent her to her room when we got home. I even went so far as to show her a cat that had run into the road. When I punish her, she is sorry for what she did, but the next time we leave a public place, she does the same thing again. I recently decided I could no longer pick her up kicking and screaming and carry her to the car. She is just too big. I have been leaving her home as much as I can while I do shopping, but I can't give up my free time forever. What can I do to control this behavior?*

A: Before I answer your question, I feel compelled to make it perfectly clear that I do not endorse having small children view flattened house pets as a means of trying to frighten them into not running into the street. This is the sort of desperate thing parents do when they're feeling exasperated.

If at age three years, eight months, your daughter is too big for you to carry to the car, then perhaps her diet needs evaluation. Lately, I've been doing considerable research on the potential health risks—including early onset of adult (type 2) diabetes—of letting children become over-weight at an early age. Let me assure you, these are not problems any responsible parent wants a child to incur. If this is indeed a problem (as opposed to you simply being a small woman of little strength), then I'd recommend an evaluation by a pediatric nutritionist.

On the issue of your daughter's fits and attempts to escape you, in situations of this sort I recommend a method I call the "dry run."

Take her to her favorite store. Go with no purpose but that of setting a disciplinary precedent. When you get to the store, look around for a while and then buy her something she wants. It is important that when you leave the store you are not carrying anything except what you bought for your daughter. When it's time to go, and she begins to scream and struggle, you put down and leave behind what you bought for her—whether or not you've already paid for it, which means it needs to be inexpensive—pick her up, carry her to the car (you can do this!), strap her in, drive her home, confine her to her room for the remainder of the day, and put her to bed early. Make sure you tell her that this is the way it's going to be from now on. The next day take her on another dry run. When you get to the store, say, "Remember yesterday? If you scream, I'm going to take you home and put you in your room. When you're in your room, I get a lot done around the house, so scream and try to run if you want to." Act very nonchalant, like it doesn't matter to you if she screams and tries to bolt.

My guess is she won't scream, but if she does, so be it. In any case, three to five dry runs ought to solve the problem. For the next three months or so, whenever you go to a store, you should remind her of "the deal" if she loses control of herself.

Q: *Our three-and-a-half-year-old son is in a mornings-only preschool. He was in the same church program last year and had lots of meltdowns, usually during group activities. He has just started preschool again, and his teacher told me today that, sure enough, he had a major meltdown. She said he was too disruptive and loud to put him in time-out, so one of the teachers took him outside and sat with him for a while. He simply doesn't get away with such behavior at home and doesn't even try it. With a new school year and more tantrums, I want to nip this in the bud. So when we got home I put him in time-out (in a chair in a corner of a room) for an hour. I explained to him that it was because of his fussiness at school. Was I right to put him in such a long time-out? How would you suggest I handle this sort of thing in the future? I'm concerned that he may be expelled from preschool.*

A: You might, if you are feeling bold, tell your son's teachers that while a short period of time-out (three to five minutes) is a generally effective punishment for this age child, it's not likely to have any effect on misbehavior that rocks the Richter scale, including major tantrums. Time-out tends to work fairly well with toddlers, but it begins to lose its disciplinary effect around three to three and a half years, especially if the child is strong-willed. It also works with children who are already well-behaved, regardless of age, but then nearly any consequence (a stern look, a rebuke, et cetera) will move an already well-behaved child back on track.

An hour in a chair is not going to damage a three-year-old's psyche. No doubt some people will cringe in horror at the idea of making a three-year-old sit in a chair for an hour, but believe me, that will do the child no harm. Keep in mind that for a consequence to have a lasting effect, it must result in the formation of a long-term memory. Therefore, Rosemond's Make It Memorable Principle: The more memorable the consequence, the more powerful the disciplinary message. (Toddlers do not have much capacity for long-term memory, which is why parents of children younger than three often report that "nothing works.")

I recommend that you and your son's teachers double-team him when he throws a classroom tantrum. His teachers should make no attempt to calm him down. Instead, as soon as a tantrum begins, they should simply remove him from the class and call you. You should go to the school as soon as possible and retrieve him. Take him home and put him in his room for the rest of the day and to bed immediately after supper. Before you begin this rehabilitation program, you might want to consider performing a mild "sterilization" procedure on your son's room: Simply remove and store his favorite playthings.

Long confinement to a relatively boring room will create a much more powerful long-term memory than will an hour in a chair. Regardless, keep in mind that "the third time is the charm." I don't mean that three applications of a consequence should be sufficient to cure the problem. Rather, most consequences will not work until they have been applied at least three times. Another way of saying the same thing: A consequence, no matter how memorable, won't work unless you work at it.

Q: *I am the single, stay-at-home mother of a three-year-old boy who is defiant and not responding to my discipline. I spank, use time-out, and take away privileges, all to no avail. He hits other children, refuses to obey me, runs away in stores, throws wild tantrums when he doesn't get his way, and so on. I take him to the bathroom and spank him, or we leave the playdate, but we always face the same issue the next time. His behavior is fantastic for his grandparents and my friends, but only when I'm not around. I can't figure out the cause of this problem, and I feel like I am beating my head against the wall. Help!*

A: To begin with, trying to figure out the cause of these behavior problems will paralyze your ability to discipline effectively. Besides, if you simply must know the cause, it is that your son, like many young children (and adults), is determined to get his own way, always. Now that we have that said, let's see what we can do about this most vexing situation.

Like most parents, you obviously believe that punishment is the essence of discipline. Not so. Effective discipline is a function of effective leadership, and the essence of leadership is proper communication. Leaders do not create disciples, people who will follow their lead, by punishing them. They create disciples through effective speech. In an instructional situation, leadership speech is brief and to the point (short and sweet), leaves nothing to the imagination (no uncertain terms), and is not accompanied by elaborate explanations.

By and large, today's parents do not give instructions to their children properly. Ending an "instruction" with "okay?" is but one example. Giving long-winded explanations (reasoning) is another. More often than not, and especially with a young child, an explanation creates the impression that the parent is trying to persuade instead of expecting the child to obey. With that in mind, my first suggestion is that you train yourself to communicate properly with your little rebel. Example: Instead of saying, "How about helping me pick up these toys, okay?" say, "I want you to pick up these toys, right now." And then, so as not to give the child someone to resist, walk away. Does this guarantee obedience? Of course not, but it significantly increases the likelihood.

The second most common parenting problem today is many parents' seeming inability to say no and stick to it in the face of the emotional hurricane that may result, especially with a young child. You probably need to discipline yourself to walk away from your son's tantrums and "never give up, never give in." Another strategy that I've found helpful with tantrums is to create a "tantrum place," to which the parent assigns the child whenever one occurs. When our daughter, a world-class tantrum thrower at this same age, had one of her meltdowns, we simply took her to the downstairs bathroom (which we identified as her very special and very own tantrum place) and told her she could come out when she was finished. That didn't stop her tantrums completely, but it completely robbed them of power.

Finally, since your friends and parents have no problem with your son, I suggest that you ask them what they make of the problems you're having with him. Ask them what, from their perspective, you are doing wrong. They probably know. Seek their guidance in learning how to handle your son's problem. In short, ask them to mentor you. They will probably welcome the opportunity to help.

In fact, I maintain that grandparents and other parents (those with well-behaved children, at least) will usually give better advice than ten of the world's greatest child psychologists.

Q: *Our son turns four soon, and he has been going through a personality change. His once sunny disposition has turned sour, and I don't know how to turn it back around. I am tired of putting up with smart comments, glaring looks, and deliberate disobedience. Please help!*

A: You can nip this behavior in the bud with my one-of-a-kind, world-famous, guaranteed successful, easy-does-it, three-ticket technique.

Create a "picture list" (stick figure drawings, if that's the extent of your artistic talent) of your son's Big Three Misbehaviors (or Big Five, but no more!). These can, and probably should, include pictorial representations of saying no when you tell him to do something, glaring at you, and calling you "monkey head" or whatever sort of head you happen to be. Post this list on the refrigerator. Then cut three tickets out of colored construction paper and hang them on the refrigerator with a magnetic clip.

Next, select a suitable place for time-out—a chair in the dining room, the downstairs bathroom—that's isolated, safe, and boring; mostly boring. Purchase a kitchen timer and keep it close to the time-out place.

Your son begins every day with three tickets in the clip. Every time he lets fly with one of the misbehaviors represented in the picture list, you say, "Glaring at me [for example] is one of your pictures. That will cost you a ticket and five minutes in time-out." Take one of his tickets down and put him in time-out, setting the timer as you do. When the alarm goes off, he can get up. Upon losing his third ticket of the day, however, he goes to his room for the rest of the day and goes to bed at least an hour early. (This is by no means too much confinement for a four-year-old.) He can come out of his room to use the bathroom, eat meals with the family (if he's well-behaved), and go with you when you need to go somewhere. But when he's home, he's in his room.

Now, the most important ingredient in the recipe: Consistency. This will work only if you enforce dispassionately. If you give reminders, threats, warnings, and second chances, you might as well tear the whole thing up, throw the timer away, and resign yourself to living with a brat for the next fourteen years.

Q: *I take care of a nearly four-year-old boy whose parents both work. For reasons his parents are at a loss to explain, he has developed a habit of cursing when he becomes upset. He does not say anything vulgar yet but will burst out with "damn!" or "hell!" when something doesn't go his way. His parents say they have talked to him about his language, but it keeps getting worse. They have given me permission to punish him, but I'm not sure what is the best approach. What are your suggestions?*

A: As you are well aware, a child does not acquire a vocabulary of this sort in a vacuum. He is mimicking an adult, an older child, or a character on some television program he is allowed to watch. If the nefarious influence is not in your home (and I doubt you would have asked me this question if it was), then it is something his parents are capable of identifying and eliminating. I don't think they are being completely forthright with you, in which case whatever you do to curb this language in your home will be undone when the little fellow is not in your care. Perhaps you can suggest to the parents, without implying that they themselves are the influence in question, that they make an all-out effort to determine where this language is coming from and eliminate it at its source.

On days when he is in your care, I would recommend a variation on my "ticket" technique, which is actually a modification of the old Boy Scout demerit system. Using a magnetic clip, affix three tickets—rectangles of colored construction paper—to the refrigerator. On any given day, the first time this guy curses, he loses a ticket and must sit in an isolated time-out area for ten minutes. The second time, he loses a second ticket and sits for twenty minutes. The third such incident results in the loss of the last ticket as well as a thirty-minute period of time-out.

But that's not all. Each ticket lost represents a privilege at home, something he looks forward to doing in the late afternoon or early evening. So when he loses the first ticket, he might lose the privilege of being able to play outside when he gets home. The second ticket might represent watching television, and the third might represent his normal bedtime. If he loses all three tickets at your house (which he's likely to do for several days at least), when he arrives home he cannot play outside or watch any television, and he would be put to bed at least one hour early. The combination of punishments at your house (ever-increasing periods of time-out) and corresponding punishments at home builds a bridge of communication and consequences between the two environments. If both you and his parents manage the system properly, meaning consistently and dispassionately, then I predict he will quickly learn to contain his exclamatory outbursts.

However, actually correcting the problem will require that his parents ferret out and eliminate whatever disreputable influence has caused this behavior.

Q: *Our almost nine-year-old daughter has been, for the most part, a great child. Recently, however, we have had small incidents where she has lied to us. Yesterday, for example, I asked, "Are you chewing gum?" Even though it was obvious, she denied it. We went back and forth several times before she finally admitted it and spit it out. Her lying seems to be worsening, and it worries us. Why is she doing this, and is there some way of nipping this in the bud?*

A: Your daughter is lying to you because you ask a question when you already know the answer. In this game of cat and mouse, the mouse always sets the ground rules. She steals the cheese (the truth); then she taunts you with it, and you start chasing her around the house. Even though you eventually catch her and take the cheese away, the game is exciting and as addictive as any other form of gambling.

The way to nip this in the bud is to apply the adage "Ask them no questions and they will tell you no lies." Instead of asking a question to which you know the answer, make a declarative statement and follow it with an authoritative instruction. Using your example, instead of asking your daughter if she's chewing gum, say, "You're chewing gum. Get rid of it." With this declare-instruct approach, you maintain constant control of the cheese, thus preempting the game and the debilitating addiction that inevitably follows.

Q: *My thirteen-year-old son waits until the last possible moment to begin doing his homework. He no longer has a set bedtime, but he must be in his bedroom after nine in the evening. It doesn't matter how much homework he has or even whether he has a test the next day, he doesn't crack a book until he's in his room. I've talked myself blue in the face about the importance of making* *good grades and the fact that he simply can't be doing his best if he does home-work when he's tired, but he says his grades are good enough (mostly B's with an occasional A) and I should let him make this decision. This is driving me nuts! What can I do to get him to do his homework at a decent hour?*

A: Nothing, apparently. Furthermore, I can't solve this problem for you. No, I *won't* solve this problem for you. I agree with your son. He should be allowed to make this decision. I'd suggest, therefore, that you do yourself a favor and abandon this issue forever. You're obviously causing yourself a lot of unnecessary aggravation and being a certifiable pest in the process.

As I point out in my book *Teen-Proofing*, the biggest and most frequent mistake made by responsible, well-intentioned parents of teens is the attempt to micromanage. You have to micromanage an infant or a toddler, and you might be able to micromanage a preschool or school-age child (nonetheless, I don't recommend it), but you cannot micromanage a teen without creating more problems than you solve. In fact, I'll go a step further and say that the attempt to micromanage a teen will solve abso-lutely no problems and is likely to create a slew of 'em.

Your obsessive concern about when your son does his homework falls into this perilous category. Do you really think he's going to get better grades if he does his homework when you want him to? I think it's more likely that if you manage to force him to do his homework under your eagle-eyed supervision in the afternoon or early evening, he will rush through it, in which case his grades will drop. Why? Because you have given him a good reason to prove you wrong.

Instead of trying to make your son do his homework when you think he should, give him permission to learn—the hard way if necessary—how to manage his own time. Your job here is not to manage his time for him but to demonstrate that choices result in consequences. Good choices result in good consequences (better grades, more freedom), and bad choices result in undesirable consequences (poor grades, restrictions on his freedom). For the time being, his grades are not a problem, but that may change when he enters high school and academic demands increase, giving you the opportunity to be the agent of reality. In the meantime, take a load off your shoulders and find a more constructive outlet for all that well-intentioned energy.

Q: *My fourteen-year-old daughter is driving me nuts! Every single time I refuse to let her do something or give her something she wants, she starts an argument. Then she wants the last word. I explain, reexplain, and explain some more. I even try to compromise with her, but that doesn't suit her either. Only giving in on my part will shut her up. Is there a solution short of sending her to a boarding school for the next four years?*

A: Yes, but before you can solve this problem you must emerge from your cocoon of denial and admit that you, not your daughter, have created this mess. It is not her hormones, or her age, or some innate hardheadedness or strength of will that propels these arguments. Rather, it is your well-intentioned desire to explain yourself to her. In so doing, you fling wide the door to argument, which she charges through before you can shut it. Then you blame her for taking the opportunity you presented.

Bringing an end to these nonproductive episodes will require that you give your daughter the last word. That's right! You can win the last word only with someone who will give reasonable consideration to your point of view. Since your daughter (a child) cannot begin to understand your point of view (an adult's), you cannot win the last word in any conflict with her. Besides, has your daughter ever agreed with one of your explanations? No, and she never will. Fact: If a child does not like a parent's decision, the child will not like the parent's explanation either.

So, take a page from Mahatma Gandhi's famous lost work "Parenting by the Path of Least Resistance" and give your daughter the last word. Always. Here's the formula, step by step:

Step 1: When your daughter does not like a decision you have made and demands an explanation, give her one that does not require more than ten words, as "I just don't think you're old enough to do that."

Step 2: When she scoffs, screams, mocks, or otherwise demonstrates contempt for your explanation, as in "That is the dumbest reason I've ever heard!" simply agree with her. Say, "Oh, of course, if I was your age, I'd think the same thing. Yes, I remember thinking the same thing when my mother gave me explanations of that sort. You and I are a lot alike, dear daughter."

Step 3: Immediately after Step 1 or Step 2, walk away. I call this "pulling the plug on the power struggle." You simply leave the scene quickly and let your daughter stew in her own juices.

Step 4: If she comes after you and wants to badger, just say, "Oh, yes, I'd have badgered my mother too, and my mom wouldn't have changed her mind either. My mother and I are a lot alike. Just like you and me." Then, Step 3 again.

This approach drives them crazy, which is, after all, preferable to letting them drive you crazy.

Q: *Our sixteen-year-old son's room is a perpetual pigsty. Clothes, CDs, electronic equipment, magazines, and an assortment of other personal belongings are strewn everywhere. If his bed is made, it's because I made it. If his clothes are put away, it's because I put them away. When I complain, he comes back with the "it's my room, and I can do with it as I please" bit. He also points out that his door is almost always closed, which is true, but the fact that he no longer functions as a member of the family is another problem. If he's not on his computer playing fantasy video games, he's talking on the phone to his friends. Help!*

A: This business of "it's my room, blah, blah, blah" is pure, unadulterated hogwash. The room he occupies is not his, not by a long shot. It is your property, for which you are responsible, as evidenced by the fact that you pay the share of the mortgage, insurance, and utilities represented by that room. If a guest were to fall and hurt herself in that room, you, not your naïve, deluded, and most self-absorbed sixteen-year-old, would be liable.

The chair he sits in at meals is not "his" chair, to do with as he pleases, is it? He is not free to smash it to smithereens in order to rage about the injustices of the capitalist system that maintains him in the lap of luxury, is he? To borrow from the vernacular of his articulate generation, No way! I could cite numerous other examples, but I'm sure you get my drift.

Your son is not entitled. Rather, he is obligated, and he can begin expressing his obligation by maintaining his room consistent with the standard of cleanliness you have established in your home. Whether he agrees or not is irrelevant.

You're probably saying, "But, John, I have tried everything to get him to keep his room neat and orderly, and nothing has worked."

You obviously haven't read him the riot act and then put the proverbial hammer down. If you had, you wouldn't have written me about the problem because it would quickly have become family history.

The riot act: "We will no longer tolerate the mess in the room we allow you to use. From now on, you will make your bed every morning, put your clothes in their proper places, keep the floor picked up, and otherwise maintain a clean and orderly environment. If you cooperate in this, we will reciprocate by continuing to support you in the manner to which you have become accustomed. If you refuse to cooperate, then the gravy train will come to an abrupt halt."

Putting the hammer down: "To be specific, the very next time your room is a mess in any sense of the term, we are disconnecting your modem and suspending your driving privileges for a minimum of a week. To re-earn these privileges, you must keep your room neat and clean, your clothes put away properly, and the bed made every morning for seven consecutive days. The next violation will result in the same consequences but will require compliance for two weeks. Every violation thereafter will require compliance for a month. Questions?"

The combination of reading the riot act and putting the hammer down (also known as lowering the boom) constitutes a wake-up call. And make no mistake about it, you will most definitely have to put the hammer down at least twice before His Majesty wakes up and smells the coffee.

This is an example of what I call the "Godfather Principle"—to motivate rebellious children we must make them offers they can't refuse—for which we are indebted to a now-deceased Sicilian philosopher named Don Corleone.

Q: *Our nineteen-year-old son is home for the summer from college. He frequently goes out with his buddies and drinks and afterward decides to drive home. We have talked with him about selecting a designated driver, staying where he is until he's sober, or calling us to come get him. He maintains that he doesn't drink enough to impair his driving ability. We think otherwise. What can we do?*

A: Oh, this is one of the easiest questions a parent has ever asked me! I'm going to assume that a nineteen-year-old is driving on your insurance policy. Therefore, it may have occurred to you that if he is busted for driving while impaired (whether he thinks he is or not is irrelevant to the Breathalyzer) or, worse, causes an accident, you are liable. *He* won't be sued. Your insurance company will be, and if your coverage is insufficient, so will you. In either case, your insurance company will probably drop you like a hot potato. To say that new insurance will be costly is an understatement.

Your son is obviously intelligent, but he is still in the grips of adolescent invincibility disorder (AID). Like the typical adolescent, he thinks he is immune to disaster, impervious to harm, indestructible, immortal, and invisible. Therefore, talk will accomplish nothing other than to give you cases of blue-in-the-face. You cannot convince your son that his attitude is irrational. He thinks your concerns reflect lingering parental overprotection. You cannot persuade him that his behavior involves significant risk. He just thinks you're being your typical (in his mind) neurotic selves. Furthermore, it should have occurred to you that you cannot, at this point, trust him. If his back's against the wall, he is likely to say anything to get you to back off. So stop talking and *do* something. Here are your options:

1. Take your son off your insurance policy and inform him that if he wants to dance, he's going to have to pay the band, as in pay for his own policy. The simple fact is, a child (and your son is obviously still a child) is more likely to take care of that for which he has toiled. He has no job? Too bad. Perhaps he needs to reassess his priorities.

2. If you are the owners of record, sell the car he drives. Don't discuss it with him first or warn him, just sell it.

3. Emancipate him, completely, which means you also effect Option 1.

4. The next time your son goes out with his buddies, have a police officer waiting at the house when he comes home. Said officer could administer a Breathalyzer test and, if it's positive, arrest your son for driving while impaired. When he asks why, tell him that you will not aid and abet dangerous criminal behavior. Period.

5. If none of these suggestions is to your liking—in other words, if you simply cannot bring yourself to dispense tough love—then look the other way and pray a lot.

Q: *My two sons are seven and four. When their cousins of the same ages come over, they all go down to our basement to play. Invariably within thirty minutes my younger son will come upstairs crying because his older brother is being mean to him, excluding him from games, and causing the cousins to gang up against him. I find myself going down to the basement every half hour to settle one of these disputes, but I'd like to solve the problem once and for all. What can you suggest?*

A: You're absolutely right. Settling one of these conflicts does not solve the problem. In fact, as you've discovered, settling 1,358,495 of these disputes will not solve the problem. Your willingness to serve as a mediator is making matters worse. Unwittingly, by coming to your younger son's rescue, you cause the other boys to resent him and want to get back at him. When they do, he cries, you rescue again, again they resent, and it's just a matter of time before another episode occurs.

Some experts might tell you to ignore all this. That's unrealistic. I couldn't ignore it. In fact, I'd be every bit as irritated as you are. Other experts might say, "Let them work it out." Not me. It may take the children years to work this out. Meanwhile, you will slowly become a prime candidate for the Funny Farm. I say you should help the boys work it out.

The secret to helping them do this is to transfer the emotional burden of this problem—the monkey of the problem, so to speak—from your back to your sons'. Leave the cousins out of this. They are guests in your home.

Here's how you do it: The next time the cousins come over to play, let only one of your sons down to the basement to play with them. Flip a coin to determine who it will be.

Say, "Obviously you both cannot go down to the basement with your cousins at the same time without causing a problem. I'm tired of the provoking, and I'm tired of the crying, so only one of you goes down today. And this is the way it's going to be for quite some time. Today I'm going to flip a coin to determine who goes down, who stays up. Next time the cousins come over, the child who stayed upstairs today is allowed downstairs, and the child who was allowed downstairs today will be upstairs. Are you ready? Heads is older, tails is younger. Here goes!"

Bada bing, bada boom! The problem is solved. If the weather is nice enough for them to go outside, let only the son whose turn it is to be in the basement out with the cousins. This causes both boys to become highly motivated to solve the problem, and they will. Maintain this policy over the next four times the cousins come over. Then, when each of your sons has experienced forced exclusion twice, ask them right before the cousins show up, "Do I need to keep one of you upstairs today?" I don't have to tell you what the answer will be. Let them both play with the cousins until a problem develops, then separate the son who would have been excluded that day.

This strategy forces the boys to solve the problem, something you cannot do. But before your sons can tame the monkey of the problem, it must be on *their* backs.

3

Fundamental Parenting Principle Three

*It's About Respecting Others,
Not High Self-Esteem*

Blessed are the meek, for they will inherit the earth.

—Matthew 5:5

I was about to speak at an elementary school in Alabama when my mind fell under the sway of a certain biological imperative. Upon walking into the boys' restroom (no men on faculty equaled no men's restroom), I couldn't help but notice a computer-generated banner stretched above the mirror on which was printed, in large, hand-colored letters:

> **You are now looking at one of the most special people in the whole wide world!**

I knew the special person in question wasn't me, so I assumed this was what the school's principal and teachers wanted each and every child in the school to believe. No one can fault the intention behind such a banner. The problem lies in the fact that it simply isn't true. The truth is, no one is "special." By virtue of being human, each person is full of flaws that exert powerful tugs on behavior. It is supremely easy to give in to one's own self-centered nature, to justify outbursts of hurtful anger, selfishness, jealousy, greed, and so on. Keeping the demons within under control requires effort. Good parenting—a balance of unconditional love and firm, unconditional discipline—equips a child to make and maintain that effort (with reasonable success). Above all else, good parenting endows the child with a sense of social obligation (respect for others) strong enough to suppress his or her self-centered impulses (most of the time). The child develops self-respect as a consequence of parents guiding him to respect others, *not* telling him he's special.

You think your child is special? That's perfectly all right. The difference between feeling that your child is special to *you* and leading her to believe she *is* special in the universal sense is apples and coconuts. There's something dreadfully wrong, in fact, with a parent who is devoid of the feeling that his or her children are special. But "You're very special to me" is a far cry from "You're one of the most special people in the whole wide world!"

Should a child be told that he is competent and capable of great things, that he can overcome adversity and rise admirably to a challenge? Of course. But none of that is synonymous with leading a child to believe that he is a cut above everyone else. A child who thinks he's special in that sense is highly likely to think he's also deserving of special things, special privileges, being first in line, having the best bicycle, and so on. Is it all right for a child to feel pride in his accomplishments? Yes, but that's different from being "prideful," as in vain and egotistical. Pride is authentic only when the person in question is fundamentally humble. Authentic pride, furthermore, is directed *not* at the self but at specific accomplishments.

The notion reflected on that banner is also contrary to a child's best interests. Every parent should want to produce children who are socially charming. I ask you to consider: Is an adult who obviously thinks he or she is "one of the most special people in the whole wide world" charming? Of course not! A person who believes that about himself is, well, obnoxious. Why then are adults in America encouraging children to believe they are all special?

Beginning in the 1960s, professional parenting experts began telling parents to direct their energies toward nurturing something they called "self-esteem." I've been a critic of this idea for most of the twenty-six years I've been writing my nationally syndicated newspaper column. Invariably when I write on the subject, people write me back suggesting that I misunderstand what self-esteem is all about. They point out that true self-esteem is a feeling of self-worth based on accomplishments—what I earlier termed *authentic pride*. I understand the argument they're making, but it turns on itself. If we're talking about not the *self* but the good things the self *does*, then let's not call it *self*-esteem, and let's get rid of the word *esteem* as well. After all, *esteem* means "worship." If "self-worship" is really not what is meant by the term, then let's call it something else. We don't have to invent a new term here, because the word *responsible* will more than suffice.

The world would be a better, steadily improving place if adults concentrated on simply teaching children to be responsible—to have compassion and respect for others (social responsibility), to do their best (task responsibility), and to do the right thing even when no one else is watching (personal responsibility).

Parents can produce children who fit this description by applying the following fairly old-fashioned five child-rearing principles:

1. *Praise the act, not the child.* More than thirty years ago, Rudolf Dreikurs, the author of *Children: The Challenge*, warned parents against the use of "evaluative praise," by which he meant praise that was directed at the child rather than at some specific accomplishment. Saying to a child, "You're a wonderful little boy!" is as hurtful to the child's self-concept as saying, "You're a little brat!" What the parent or teacher really means and should really say is "You did a great job on this and you should be proud."

2. *Praise conservatively.* Too much praise, as well as praise that is effusive, can create a powerful dependency. The child who asks for praise constantly, who always seems to need reassurance that she's

doing a good job or the right thing, has usually received praise that was excessive and unwarranted. In the literal sense, the child has become addicted to regular doses of praise. Yes, she's insecure, because she feels secure only when an adult is praising her. But this is not the same as insecure because you're unsure of your parents' love since they *never* praise. A child who receives no praise doesn't go looking for it.

3. *Help your children learn they are capable of standing on their own two feet by not letting them stand on yours.* Do for your children only what they cannot do for themselves and always remember that children usually underestimate their ability. Their cries for help are often no more than knee-jerk responses to frustration. It is a parent's job to bring out the best in his or her kids. Often the best way of doing so is simply to say no. Learning to stand on one's own feet is not supposed to be easy. In fact, the only people who ever truly make it are people who are able to hang tough in the face of frustrating circumstances. As weight lifters say, "No pain, no gain."

4. *Teach your children that choices result in consequences.* When your children misbehave, punish. Show them by example, which is how children learn, that one must pay a price for misbehavior, that it is not ever "free." Another way of saying the same thing: When a child does something bad, he should be made to feel bad about it. This is how conscience—the ultimate behavioral "governor"—develops. By contrast, when your child behaves well, acknowledge his accomplishment with moderate praise. Not rewards or lavish praise but something simple like "You did well. I'm mighty proud of you."

5. *Teach your children good manners.* In the process of learning to say "please," "thank you," and "I'm sorry," learning *not* to interrupt conversations, and so on, children acquire sensitivity for other people's feelings, without which respect for others is impossible.

Above all else, we need to emphasize humility in the child-rearing equation. After all, there is no one more obnoxious than someone who thinks he's special, and no one more charming than a person who's more interested in you than in having you know about him.

The idea that high self-esteem is good has caused untold damage to our culture. Recent research findings support my position. Consider:

- In a recent international academic competition, American high school students came in dead last. They tended to believe, however, that they'd done really well. Korean students, who ranked near the top, were inclined to believe they hadn't done very well at all. It's beginning to look as if good self-esteem may be more of a hindrance than a help to actual achievement. It also looks as if high self-esteem produces fantastic thinking about one's performance, whereas humility (still a value in Asia) lends itself to higher achievement.
- After studying high self-esteem in children, two research psychologists recently concluded that children with inflated feelings of worth which were unsupported by real accomplishment were prone, when their precarious self-image was threatened, to become aggressive or even violent.
- Lending support to the preceding finding, researchers have found that violent criminals doing long-term sentences in maximum-security prisons were likely to score significantly higher on a measure of self-esteem than the average law-abiding good citizen.

The experts were wrong in saying that high self-esteem would lead to better grades and better behavior. In fact, the research is fairly conclusive that people who are modest and humble, and who possess a healthy capacity for self-effacement, are not just the nicest people to be around but also exemplars of a good work ethic, community-mindedness, empathy, and social compassion. In short, they are the people most likely to lend you a helping hand if they see that you need one.

I encourage the well-intentioned principal of that Alabama elementary school to tear down the "You're special" banners and replace them with banners that read "Do something special for someone else today, just because you should."

Violent Pride

Who had higher self-esteem, Mahatma Gandhi or Adolf Hitler? Columbine High School's 1999 valedictorian or the two CHS students who, in April of that year, killed a teacher, twelve fellow students, and then themselves? Albert Einstein or Adolf Eichmann? Popeye or Bluto?

With respect to each pair, if you picked the first person, you're wrong. In each case the bad guy, not the good guy, is infected with the virus of high self-esteem. So says Dr. Roy F. Baumeister, whose article "Violent Pride," featured in the April 2001 issue of *Scientific American*, should be required reading for every school board member, principal, teacher, therapist, and parent in America. Baumeister, a social scientist at Florida State University, has studied the relationship between aggression and self-esteem for more than a decade. His findings completely explode the self-esteem mythology that has driven American parenting and education for more than a quarter century and explain why, in the bad old days, when parents and teachers reinforced humility and modesty rather than false pride, America's kids were much better behaved and far less prone to violent outbursts.

People with high self-esteem, says Baumeister, are likely to respond aggressively when their inflated view of themselves is threatened by criticism or perceived insult or when someone obstructs their need for gratification. Gang members have high self-esteem. So do spouse abusers. In short, the higher one's self-esteem, the lower one's self-control.

Doesn't it make perfect sense that the higher one's opinion of oneself, the less regard one has for others? Doesn't it make perfect common sense that humble, modest people possess a more functional sense of social responsibility than people who think they are social elites? Doesn't it make perfect sense that a school teeming with kids who've been repeatedly told there is nothing about themselves that requires improvement is not as safe as a school populated with kids whose teachers and parents set high expectations, dispense criticism when it's due, and are intolerant of egotistic behavior? These days, that description is virtually exclusive to schools supported by religious denominations—generally speaking, the safest schools in America.

Baumeister makes clear that he finds no fault with performance-based self-esteem, the feeling that one is capable of mustering whatever it takes to overcome challenge and adversity (I call this self-competence). His warnings are aimed at the brand of self-esteem that develops when parents and teachers dispense praise, reward, and good grades unconditionally— i.e., irrespective of merit. Unfortunately, it's the latter sort that today's kids tend to be "high" on.

Pride cometh before a fall, or so the saying goes. As Baumeister's research demonstrates, the people who end up taking the falls are often those who have run-ins with the prideful.

Slowly but surely, the lid is coming off the self-esteem can of worms. According to research published in the November 2001 issue of *Personality and Social Psychology Review*, while self-esteem among America's youth has been on the rise for the last thirty years, accomplishment and responsible decision making have been on the decline. The sort of self-esteem many of America's kids are bloated on is not based on a realistic appraisal of their strengths and weaknesses; therefore, it does not lead to accomplishment. Since it is based on unconditional, uncritical acceptance of whatever they do and think, it leads to mediocrity.

One of the researchers, Professor Jean Twenge of San Diego State University, in an interview with Reuters Health, laid much of the blame on America's public schools, where teachers are often forbidden to send any negative (i.e., critical) messages to children (including bad grades for bad work), and children are often encouraged to write and repeat affirmations of the "I'm special no matter what" variety. "Children should be praised," Twenge said, "but only when the praise has a basis in fact."

Contrary to psychological myth, praise by itself does not produce high achievement. High expectations coupled with accurate, supportive feedback produce high achievement that merits praise, which leads to positive self-assessment: confidence in one's own ability to surmount challenge. The realization that one is a competent human being is addicting in the positive sense. A person who has proven to himself or herself that he or she is competent will seek other opportunities to experience that same "rush."

The problem, as this research illuminates, is that America's schools have lowered expectations, dramatically so, for more than thirty years. At the same time, they have upped the level of positive reinforcement. The fact is, low expectations accompanied by inaccurate positive feedback (i.e., unconditional praise, inflated grades) produce low achievement and high self-esteem. According to Twenge, the high self-esteem in question—counterfeit positive self-assessment—sets children up for disappointment.

The further problem is that these high-self-esteem kids, having been given something for nothing, are likely to enter adulthood believing the whole world is a perpetual entitlement program designed with them in mind. Addicted not to achievement but to entitlement, they may expect the same treatment from spouses, employers, the legal system, and society in general. In fact, corporate managers across the country consistently tell me this is exactly the problem they're having with young employees. Some of these high-self-esteemers become depressed; others attempt to get what they think they deserve by engaging in antisocial behavior, including stealing from their employers.

"So, John," you may be thinking, "do you believe in low self-esteem?"

No, I actually believe in *no* self-esteem. Once upon a not-so-long-ago time, lack of self-esteem was known as humility and modesty. I believe in those old-fashioned virtues; there's nothing so charming as a humble, modest individual, whether child or adult.

For more than a generation, mental health professionals have urged parents and teachers to promote high self-esteem in children. They are now saying they intended all along for self-esteem to be connected to accomplishments. Wrong. The intent all along was for children to feel like demigods *regardless* of accomplishment. In fact, if a child failed at something, adults were supposed to pretend he had succeeded; if he lost, adults were supposed to pretend he'd won; if he misbehaved, adults were to look the other way, ensuring he wouldn't feel bad about what he'd done. Punishment of any sort lowered self-esteem, the experts said, and so did being told what to do. Families were to be "democratic" (i.e., socialist microcosms). Parents were to praise children for every little thing, which clearly meant that accomplishment mattered little.

High self-esteem is a problem, if not for the individual who is infected with it, then certainly for the rest of us. By age two, the child of even marginally competent parents has very high self-esteem. She has every right to believe that, as her parents have tended to do since the day she was born, the world revolves around her and always will. What she wants, she thinks she deserves, and the ends justify the means. That describes the criminal mentality, and indeed, toddlers are little criminals. They lie, steal, hit, bite, disdain authority, have little regard for rules or tolerance for frustration, and crave instant gratification. Oh, they're cute too, but then your average criminal can be charming when he wants to be.

The high self-esteem of the toddler is an illness that needs to be cured. This is by no means a radical idea, and until fairly recently parents did exactly that. How? With a combination of powerful discipline and equally powerful love.

Unfortunately, this sort of parenting fell by the wayside beginning in the 1960s. Following expert advice, American parents stopped curing self-esteem and began promoting it instead. The trendsetter was the American public school, whose primary mission became that of purveying "I feel special" mantras. It is certainly no coincidence that since high self-esteem became the touchstone of American child rearing, rates of child and teen violence have skyrocketed. The perpetual toddler is as the perpetual toddler does.

Self-Respect Versus "I'm Special!"

I have often said that the desired goal should be self-respect, not self-esteem. "Well, John," a fellow recently said, "I think you're mincing words. You're really talking about the same thing."

The fellow's challenge reflects the fact that our national obsession with attaining the supposed cure-all of high self-esteem (and making sure our children acquire it in abundance) has resulted in semantic confusion. People tend to think that self-confidence, self-respect, and self-esteem are one and the same. The notion that true self-esteem is acquired not by being praised a lot but through accomplishment is also common. Let's examine these arguments.

If self-esteem is truly all about accomplishment, then it is a decidedly un-American notion, because it means that those who are not capable of much accomplishment are not due a lot of self-esteem. The meritocracy of self-esteem should not appeal to anyone other than people with high self-esteem, who tend, so the research says, to delight in the notion that they are a cut above the rest of us.

As for self-esteem and self-confidence being one and the same, the research says that people with high self-esteem do not seem able to accurately assess their own abilities. They tend to think they are good, or capable of being good, at everything. It is simply not functional to be confident across the board. Rather, it is smart to know what situations one would do best to avoid and when to ask for help. That most sensible trait is not characteristic of people with high opinions of themselves.

Which brings us to the difference between self-respect and self-esteem. The former is acquired as a consequence of giving respect away, of doing things for others. The more respect for others goes around, the more self-respect comes around. Self-esteem, by contrast, is acquired as a consequence of people doing things for you—praising you indiscriminately, creating artificial success experiences for you, giving you material things, and generally treating you like the potentate we all, deep inside, want to be. People with high self-respect feel a sense of obligation to others. People with high self-esteem feel that others are obligated to them. They feel entitled, and the feeling that one is entitled leads directly to all manner of rude, ill-mannered, antisocial behavior—lying, bullying, temper tantrums, and worse. Sounds like some children you know? Maybe some adults?

No, the difference between self-esteem and self-respect is not a mere matter of words. The very real difference produces two entirely different sorts of people, and therefore two entirely different cultures. If you've traveled abroad to any significant degree, then you know exactly what I mean.

Children Abroad

When a break in my generally nonstop speaking schedule opened in October 2003, Willie and I took the opportunity to go to London. We took in the National Gallery and the British Museum, rode the Eye, which is the world's largest Ferris wheel, shopped at Harrods, ate at fine restaurants, and walked more than we had in years. London is a splendid place, and we had a splendid time.

The first morning, I opened the London *Times* and read it with coffee and scones. Turning to the *Times'* magazine supplement, I was immediately struck by the headline, OUR CHILDREN ARE OUT OF CONTROL! It seemed that English nannies, many of whom are imported from Eastern Europe, regarded their charges as generally obnoxious, disrespectful, and disobedient—brats.

I was prepared, therefore, to witness lots of evidence of this disciplinary debacle. Over the next six days, Willie and I were around lots of English children in a variety of situations. Never once did we see a child misbehave in any noticeable manner. Never once did we hear a child talk belligerently, demandingly, or defiantly to a parent. Never once did we hear a child, even a toddler, throw a tantrum in a store. Where were the "out of control" children? I concluded that Einstein was correct—everything is relative.

At one point Willie and I stepped out of Selfridges department store onto busy Oxford Street. The sidewalk was crowded, and I inadvertently bumped into a girl of age six or seven, who was walking arm in arm with a man I presume was her father. I've bumped into American children in crowded places. They generally look up at you with an annoyed expression. In any case, the last time I have heard "excuse me" from an American child was in 1983, if memory serves me well.

This little English sweetie looked up at me and without hesitation said, "I'm so sorry." I stood there in shock. By the time I was able to form the words "No, *I'm* sorry," she and her father had disappeared into the crowd. They probably went home and talked about how rude American tourists can be.

One night Willie and I took in *Mamma Mia*, the musical based on the songs of ABBA. Coming out of the theater, neither of us knew the direction to our hotel, and every cab we saw had occupants. About two blocks from the theater, I stopped to ask a group of teenagers—they looked sort of "punkish"—for directions. They were most concerned and most polite, and they had to have known, immediately, that we were American.

English parents are not out of control either. Walking through Hyde Park, Willie and I came upon several groups of primary school children playing competitive soccer. They were in uniform, and the games were obviously intense. Let me emphasize, however, that these games were taking place in the late afternoon, after school. Each game was attended by no more than five adults—mostly coaches and officials—and even they seemed a bit uninterested.

There was a time in the USA when parents were not out of control. In 1959, the only year I played Little League baseball, the only adults present at any of our games were the coaches and the umpires; therefore, the games were fun. Today's children, I'm convinced, don't know what fun is because it's not fun when adults are micromanaging and screaming on the sidelines.

The *Times* had it all wrong. From the point of view of someone from Eastern Europe, where the traditional extended family is still the norm and the gene pool is curiously deficient in those genes that supposedly cause attention deficit hyperactivity disorder and childhood-onset bipolar disorder, I'm sure English children, especially the ones with parents who can afford nannies, are "out of control." But from the point of view of this observer of American parenting, the typical English child is nothing short of charming.

Spoiled, As in Rotten

In August 2001, I was asked to appear on CNN's *TalkBack Live*, where the topic was America's spoiled children. Earlier that month *Time* magazine made the belated discovery ("Who's in Charge Here?" August 6, 2001) that America's kids are given too much in every conceivable way, so the media were proceeding to beat the matter to death. Then everyone went back to business as usual. In other words, America's kids had nothing to worry about.

Let's face it, parents read these articles and watch these programs and think to themselves, "Oh! Isn't it awful that so many parents spoil their children!" never realizing the articles and programs are about them.

I think the problem is with the word *spoiled*. It is synonymous with *rotten*, which means being in a state of decay—i.e., smelling bad. Perhaps if we renamed the problem, calling it something that isn't so putrid, parents would be willing to admit they are creating it and change their ways. With that in mind, I propose changing the term *spoiled children* to *ungrateful, demanding, petulant brats*. The question then becomes, Are you raising an ungrateful, demanding, petulant brat (UDPB)?

If you're having trouble figuring it out, here's a quick self-test. Answer each question simply true or false:

1. When I buy my child something he wants but does not need—a new toy, for example—he acts like it's about time I did something for him.

2. If I don't do what my child wants me to do, she is likely to cry and scream at me that I'm a bad parent.

3. I have to virtually get down on my knees and beg my child to accept any responsibility at all, and even then it's iffy.

Okay, if you answered true to even one of these questions, you have a UDPB. Why does just one true qualify a child? Because one true means you should have answered true to the other two questions but didn't because, like most American parents, you're in heavy denial concerning your child.

So what would a non-UDPB act like? My church's newsletter recently contained a letter to the congregation from a young man who grew up in the church and was giving a year of his life to the service of disadvantaged children at an orphanage in Honduras. For starters, the young man in question, albeit from a family of considerable means, was and is definitely *not* a UDPB.

He writes:

The second image that struck me was watching a child and a dog fight over what looked to be a chicken carcass. The child won and tore at it greedily. I wish I could paint with words what the city is like. However, the actual orphanage is heaven for these children. Never in my life have I met more respectful and grateful children. A far cry from what I saw growing up in [a small eastern U.S. city]. These children know how lucky they are to have even the opportunity to take responsibility for their lives—an outlook many children in the States lack.

Amen. I'm sure every American parent, if asked, would say they want their children to be respectful and grateful. To walk that talk is very simple, actually. This young man has put his finger on the key to raising a non-UDPB. If you want your child to be grateful and respectful, don't give him or her a lot. Say no more than you say yes—a lot more, in fact. At least ten noes to every yes is my suggestion. And while you're at it, be a model of frugality, patience, and service to others. Children are more impressed, in every sense of the term, by someone who serves others than by someone who serves them. Put your children to work around the house, and work alongside them. Our young missionary rises at the crack of dawn every morning and goes to work with the boys who live in the orphanage. Together they slop hogs, shovel manure, and weed fields by hand until it's time for supper, at which point they all bow their heads and thank the Good Lord for each and every small blessing in their lives.

Rich lives, indeed.

Questions?

Q: *My daughter will be seven soon. She is not an extremely social child and chooses to have only three or four friends. For her birthday she wants to invite four children she likes, but not three other children with whom she has played and whose mothers are my friends. I feel strongly that she should invite these three children too. If they hear about the party (which is likely), their feelings—and their moms'—will be hurt, I'm sure. My explanations have fallen on deaf ears. My daughter absolutely refuses to invite them. So I gave her a choice: party with these three included or no party. She quickly said, "No party, thank you." Did I do the right thing, or should I have let her decide whom to invite to her party without my interference?*

A: Yes, you did the right thing, and for that I hereby bestow upon you Rosemond's Seldom Given Meanie Meanie Meanie Award. A child should not be allowed to use a party as a platform for selfish, mean-spirited, narcissistic behavior. Unfortunately, many parents allow their children's birthday parties to be stages for exactly that sort of obnoxious performance. A celebration of one's birthday is a time to be grateful, selfless, generous. You wanted your daughter to include, not exclude; to open her heart, not close it. You were absolutely, positively, indisputably right. Clearly, your daughter was wrong, wrong, and more wrong. You explained your position. Your daughter stuck to her guns. You tried more persuasion. She stuck to her guns. At that point, you could have either laid down the law or caved in. To your everlasting credit, you laid down the law. Your daughter still stuck to her guns. Now you stick to yours!

Q: *My sister and her husband recently threw a birthday party for their five-year-old daughter that included pony rides, a visit from Cinderella (who gave each child a magic gift), a cake that rivaled my wedding cake, and needless to say, a glut of expensive gifts, including a doll that looked just like her and her first diamond. At one point, I thought they were going to put her on a throne and parade her through town. Our five-year-old daughter attended and now thinks that we should throw an equally lavish bash for her next birthday. Your thoughts, please.*

A: I am a certified fuddy-dud on the subject of children's birthday parties. Once upon a time not so long ago, these tended to be modest affairs, but that was before the Age of the Almighty Child. Sometimes, the child's birthday party consisted simply of a cake baked that day by the child's mother and served after the evening meal. Family members who lived in town arrived in time to partake of this dessert, everyone sang "Happy Birthday to You," and the child was the recipient of several equally modest gifts. But again, that was when a child was a child, not a demigod.

When birthday parties were modest affairs, children behaved in a far more civil fashion than is generally the case today. They were not encouraged to believe "it" was all about them; therefore, they developed a sense of respect and obligation toward others. Ergo, better behavior. Modest birthday parties certainly helped the child keep his or her place in the overall scheme of things in a reasonably sane perspective.

Times have changed. Back then, modesty in all things was a virtue. For one thing, you didn't brag about your children, or dote on them. Or lavish them with finery. It was generally known, back then, that high self-esteem was not a solution, it was the problem. Today's parents are convinced that the more they can do for their children's self-esteem, the better. A five-thousand-dollar birthday party for a five-year-old? No price is too great!

Needless to say, I am in favor of the modest, family-only birthday party. If other children are to be invited, keep it small and simple. Disallow gifts. In fact, I like the idea of the birthday child giving a small thank-you gift to each child he invites. Even require the child to pay for these gifts himself. That will surely keep the numbers down. Serve a healthy dessert, and send the other kids (if there are any) packing after a game of pin the tail on the donkey or blindman's bluff.

Once upon a time, children were satisfied with modest birthday parties. It's a pity they've been taught to expect so much more. Take it from someone who's been there, done that: Desire for things one doesn't need is not consistent with happiness.

Q: *My husband's sister is attractive, highly intelligent, and successful. Unfortunately, she is thoroughly self-absorbed. Almost every conversation with her eventually comes back to how beautiful and incredibly talented she is. If she has a conflict with someone, it's because he or she is jealous. I'm worried because people tell me my six-year-old daughter is a lot like her aunt. They mean well (her aunt is also gregarious and charming), but I'm beginning to see that my daughter is also somewhat self-absorbed. When she acts this way, I lecture and make her apologize. Is it possible that she has inherited this personality trait from her father's side of the family? Also, is it all right to tell a six-year-old that she's being selfish and inconsiderate, or is that too harsh?*

A: No, your daughter hasn't inherited her aunt's narcissism. It's important to distinguish between personality, which is like a template one is born with, and character, which is the stuff that slowly fills in the template. Research suggests that personality traits may be inherited, but not character. For example, the fact that your sister-in-law is outgoing—a personality characteristic—may have genetic origins, but her self-centeredness—a character trait—definitely does not.

Shaping a child's character requires a combination of powerful love and equally powerful discipline. The job is far from over by the time a child is six years old. It sounds to me like you're on the right track. Stay there.

To your second question: If telling your daughter that she's being "selfish and inconsiderate" is the truth, the whole truth, and nothing but the truth, then that's not, in and of itself, harsh. The truth sometimes hurts, but hurt of this sort can also be healing. Telling her *harshly* is another matter. When you tell her this sort of thing, keep in mind that words spoken coolly sink further into the brain than words spoken in anger.

Q: *My seven-year-old is a poor sport, gloating when he wins a game and crying when he loses. My husband's entire family shares this trait with him, so it's more than just his age. Games and competitive sports with his peers are especially problematic. When we play board games at home, he cries when he loses and makes fun of us when he wins, just like he does with his peers. By the way, my husband is coming to grips with this about himself, but he's still got a way to go.*

A: If you mean that you think your son inherited this tendency, I doubt it. Unbeknownst to the general public, the search for genetic explanations of human behavior has not panned out. In fact, studies of identical twins reared apart have debunked the notion that specific behavioral traits are passed from generation to generation through any reliable genetic mechanisms.

You're right to be concerned. His peers will not tolerate your son's poor sportsmanship much longer. The older he becomes, the more social problems this will cause, and for good reason. Poor sportsmanship is, after all, a show of self-centered disrespect for others. Whereas seven-year-olds will suffer it, ten-year-olds will not. Adults who are presently likely to regard this as simple immaturity will view it as a much more serious problem in a few years.

In short, you can't afford to waste any time. Assuming your husband shares your concerns, he should join you in a full-scale curative effort. In fact, I'd venture to say that if your son doesn't begin hearing a strong message of disapproval from his father, unilateral efforts on your part to remedy this problem will not succeed.

In my experience, there's but one effective way to handle this behavior. As soon as your son begins to gloat or get upset during a game, he should be *immediately* removed and not allowed to continue unless he apologizes to everyone—the coaches, his teammates, and the kids on the other team. If he refuses to do so, then you must take him home and confine him to his room for the rest of the day. Needless to say, his coaches must also be completely supportive of this remedy. If it's not convenient for the game to stop so your son can apologize, then you should simply take him home. Under those circumstances, before he can join the team for the next practice or game, he must apologize for his previous bad behavior.

You may be asking yourself, "Won't that embarrass him?" The answer is "Absolutely!" That is the point. Your son must be required to experience a negative emotional consequence powerful enough to cause him to begin controlling his antisocial behavior on the field.

When he displays the same sort of behavior during a game with either or both of you, you should stop the game immediately and send him to his room. He stays in his room until he produces a written apology to the two of you. This apology should be no less than one page in length and should contain an explanation of why it is wrong to gloat or get upset during games.

Apologies are good for the soul, and what's good for the soul helps children change their behavior.

4

Fundamental Parenting Principle Four

It's About Manners and Morals, Not Skills

In everything, therefore, treat people the same way you want
them to treat you, for this is the Law and the Prophets.

—Matthew 7:12

In 1997, the Dayton (Ohio) Chamber of Commerce surveyed local employers on a variety of issues. When asked what they were looking for in prospective employees, they overwhelmingly valued character over specific skills—even computer skills. They also said that it's fairly easy to find people who know how to run a computer, but finding people of good character is becoming increasingly difficult.

A few years ago I was reminded of that survey by a letter I received in response to one of my columns. It was from a woman whose husband is a professor at a well-known technical university. Here's what she had to say (emphasis is mine):

No one denies that the students currently enrolling at this school are some of the brightest and most accomplished ever to enroll, but the lack of character and self-control is frightening.

I won't deluge you with the horror stories about threatening behavior from the students or the irate phone calls from parents as to the "injustices" they have "endured" at the hands of the collegiate system. There are many who can speak to those issues far better than can I, but I do feel qualified to place a lot of the blame squarely on the parents of my generation. They have (collectively) reared a generation of children who excel as people, but who come up desperately short as human beings. These parents took their eyes off the prize. A sad commentary to be sure, but not a hasty one.

A dear friend and colleague of my husband's summed it up best. This man is one of the gentlest, most even-tempered, and most optimistic persons you will ever meet. One day last May he came into the office, exhaled a ragged sigh, and said: "I have taught here for thirty-seven years, but, you know, I have never seen such a bunch of lazy, self-serving whiners as I have encountered the past couple of semesters."

My mother raised ten children by herself. She always said that the biggest mistake people make with their children is they forget the goal is not to raise children, but to raise adults. The older I get, the more I agree.

Bright kids who lack character and self-control. Parents who, because they've forgotten that the goal is to raise adults, not children, raise perpetual children—successful people who come up short as human beings.

Today's parents have convinced themselves that providing opportunities for their children to learn specific skills—most notably, computer literacy—is the crux of responsible parenting. Not only is that not true (notwithstanding that certain skills, like reading, are absolutely essential) but this obsession with raising the most savvy kids on the block is getting in the way of an education in good character. If you don't believe me, here are the words of another corporate manager, in response to the same column:

"One of my best employees was a young man who had no computer experience but had a good deal of personal integrity and honesty. We taught him what he needed to know, and he is today quite successful in his new job as an inventory administrator."

The following manager didn't know anything about computers until well into adulthood. Now she's a self-described geek who wrote, "My point is I don't think it is important for kids to have all this exposure to computers to be successful in either life or computers. In fact, I know it isn't, because I am living proof of it."

Right! You can teach just about any skill to people who possess good character, and they'll be a credit to your teaching. You can teach people of bad character just about any skill too, but as for them being a credit to you, well . . . Not according to people who should know.

I've said it before, and I'll say it again. Parenting isn't about today or tomorrow. It's about twenty-five years from now. Keep that in the forefront of your thinking, and you'll hardly ever go wrong.

Good Manners and Character

I once began a talk before an audience of some three hundred parents at a church in Charlotte, North Carolina, by asking, "Raise your hand if you feel it's more important for a child to have good manners than to make all A's and B's in school." I'm sure that every single person raised his or her hand. I then challenged this audience to consider that they probably spent lots more time helping their children get good grades than they did instructing them in good manners.

I asked them to remember back to their high school years. The kids with good manners, I pointed out, may not always have been the best students. Some of them, in fact, were probably regarded as nerds. But when you go back to a class reunion, I asked, do you ever learn that one of these well-mannered nerds has made a train wreck of his or her life? No, you don't. Quite the contrary, the well-mannered nerd is likely to be highly successful as an adult, even to have achieved success that no one would have predicted solely on the basis of his or her grades.

But each and every one of us, I went on to say, knows someone who was an outstanding student, academically brilliant even, who as an adult has done absolutely nothing but waste his or her talents.

I was trying to point out gently that today's parents often say one thing and do another. They know that good manners are more important than good grades, but they pay more attention to grades than to manners. It's not that they are hypocrites. It's just that today's parents tend to focus on short-term goals, like getting good grades. The long-term goal of producing a good citizen, someone who, as an adult, is both respected and respectful, tends to get lost in the short-term shuffle.

In *Toward a Meaningful Life: The Wisdom of the Rebbe Menachem Mendel Schneerson* (adapted by Simon Jacobson), the late Rabbi Schneerson, leader of the Lubavitcher movement of Hasidic Judaism for most of the last half of the twentieth century, states unequivocally that a child's character education should take priority over his academic education. In fact, the esteemed rebbe (pronounced "reb'-be") says all other educational efforts are basically meaningless unless built on the solid foundation of good character.

In the movie *Blast from the Past*, one of the characters finally realizes, as he puts it, "good manners are a way of showing respect for others," and not, as he'd previously thought, a means of calling attention to oneself. He's also discovered, he says, that good manners consist simply of doing all you can to help the people around you feel comfortable.

As attested to in both of these examples, character and manners are inseparable. Good manners are symptomatic of good character, and the linchpin of good character is respect for others, as reflected by good manners, which consist of efforts to make other people feel comfortable. That scene in *Blast from the Past* caused me to wonder if perhaps the screenwriter had read the rebbe's teachings.

Today's parents would certainly say they want their children to possess good character, but how many actually take the time to teach proper manners? Modeling the correct behavior is not enough. Teaching manners requires instruction, and instruction—whether reminding, explaining, correcting, or rehearsing—takes time. The world would definitely be a better place if parents took even half the time they spend driving their children to various extracurricular pursuits to teach proper manners instead.

Teaching manners to preschool children—the earlier the better—pays off in numerous ways. I have nothing but personal experience to support what I'm about to say, but I'll bet my life savings that good manners go hand in hand with obedience and respect for adults, doing one's best in school, and good relationships with siblings and friends. Not to mention that the well-mannered child's parents receive lots of positive feedback from other parents, teachers, and neighbors. For all those reasons, the child in question will be much happier than he or she otherwise would have been.

The first manners children should learn by their fourth birthdays are (in no particular order)

- Saying "please," "thank you," and "you're welcome" when appropriate
- Saying "I'm sorry" when they have hurt someone either physically or emotionally
- Saying "excuse me" when appropriate (but see below for when it's *not* appropriate)
- Sharing toys and other possessions freely with playmates
- Saying "Yes, ma'am (or sir)" and "No, ma'am (or sir)" when appropriate
- Not complaining about food prepared by someone else (even their mother) and set in front of them
- Not interrupting adult conversations, even with "excuse me."

I assign a lot of weight to that last one for several reasons. First, in learning not to interrupt, a child learns patience. Second, learning not to interrupt strengthens respect for adults. Third, I am highly annoyed when a child interrupts an adult conversation.

It would appear that many, if not most, of today's parents teach their children it's perfectly all right to interrupt two adults in conversation, and for any reason at all, by simply walking up and saying "Excuse me!" I gather this because when a child simply walks up and starts talking, it's usually the case that the child's parent will stop talking to me, look down at the child, and say, "What have I taught you to say?" At which point the child says, "Excuse me," and the parent begins paying attention to what the child says. I restrain myself and patiently (on the surface at least) wait for the parent to remember his or her manners.

I said as much at a talk I gave in Southern California. Later, a well-spoken gentleman from South Africa introduced himself and remarked that he too was annoyed and cynically amused by parents who tolerated their children's interruptions. He told me that in his country, one of the first things a child is taught is how to be recognized when he wants to say something. The child should walk into the general area where the adults are talking and stand a respectful distance—say, eight feet—away. Any fool, the aforementioned gentleman said, can tell the child wants to speak. When the adults reach a point where a pause in their conversation feels natural, one (the child's parent, usually) will turn to the child and say, "Yes?" at which point the child will speak.

That is exactly what I was taught as a child, and I daresay, so were most of my peers. How is it that people who were taught this important social formality—one that speaks so loudly to the quality of their overall upbringing—fail to teach it to their own kids? To answer my own question, there are two reasons:

1. Many of today's parents seem to think parenting is taking a child to a soccer game and watching from the stands. That's not parenting. Parenting is not a spectator sport, it's hands-on.

2. Today's parents are likely to expend a lot of energy doing things that have little if any long-term value to a child, and little energy doing things that are of lasting value (and would, in fact, make their job a whole lot easier in the long run). Like taking the time to teach a child—by explaining and rehearsing, for example—how to be recognized when two adults are engaged in conversation.

In that regard, I would suggest that the fellow from South Africa had the right idea. Teach your child to stand a respectful distance from adults who are talking and wait, silently and in a state of stillness, until she is acknowledged. You should gradually increase her wait until she's learned to be silent and still for upward of five minutes.

"So, what's the child to do if there's a genuine emergency?"

How about give your child a hand signal to use in such circumstances? Let's face it, what a child considers an emergency is not always an emergency or even close to it.

"And what should I do when my child interrupts, even after I've taught her the art of waiting?"

I really don't think there's a formula for that one, other than to make sure she learns that misbehavior has consequences. Put her to bed early that evening. Cancel a sleepover that's coming up. Whatever you do, make it something she'll remember!

Don't forget, when she does the right thing, tell her how proud you are.

Teaching Manners

The mother of a five-year-old recently remarked to me, somewhat apologetically, that her child was "bad" about interrupting conversations. I thought to myself, "No, your child isn't bad about interrupting; rather, you and your husband have been bad about teaching her not to interrupt." They would no doubt disagree. My experience with parents leads me to believe these two folks would respond defensively, even indignantly, to my accusation. They would say, "But every single time she interrupts, we tell her it's not right!"

That's not teaching. That's nagging, which is how most parents try to teach their children manners, and nagging only breeds ever more nagging. Eventually, nagging breeds contempt or, at the very least, a lack of respect. So, what should any parent who wants to instruct a young child in proper social decorum do about this nagging not-so-little problem?

Parents should understand that good manners are contrary to human nature. Think about it. It is not human nature to share, say "thank you," or wait your turn. It is natural to be selfish, take other people for granted, and want to be first in line. Thus, children do not outgrow bad manners. Nor do they simply absorb them by social osmosis. Good manners must be taught. Furthermore, because replacing human nature with proper behavior is akin to paddling upstream, face it, it is not easy to teach a child manners, and it requires work. Are you ready to work? Here's my Five-Point Plan for Teaching Good Manners to a Young Child:

1. Make it a project. Whenever you teach a child something new, like using the toilet, not interrupting conversations, using a spoon, or making his or her own bed, you must make it a project. You can't teach these skills haphazardly, on a catch-as-catch-can basis, and expect success. Willie and I took Jack, our then nine-year-old grandson, with us on a trip during which we made a project of proper table manners. Before each meal, we sat down with Jack and reviewed the ins and outs of proper table etiquette. We kept to the basics: waiting until everyone has their food and the blessing has been said, asking someone to pass instead of reaching, and asking to be excused instead of simply getting up. If he slipped during a meal—and because of the review, he rarely slipped—we gently reminded him of the proper behavior. Later, we made sure to tell him how proud we were of him. In other words, we kept table manners "in front of him" for three days, and three days was all it took. Actually, Jack already knew his proper table manners, he just needed a bit of polish. When teaching a manner that's never been learned, expect the "project" to last from one to two weeks.

2. Teach one manner or set of manners at a time. The younger the child, the more important this point becomes. We could reasonably expect Jack, at age nine, to remember several manners, all of which applied to one specific situation. If Jack had been four, however, we'd have made a project of only one table manner at a time. More than one would be overwhelming for a child younger than five, and that translates to lots of frustration for parents and child.

3. Rehearse important manners before occasions when they will be needed. Let's say you're trying to teach your four-year-old to look people in the eye and say "hello" when spoken to. Immediately before each situation in which that behavior will be called for, give your child practice.

4. Remind on the spot but gently. Quite simply, it is bad manners to reprimand a child sternly or loudly when other adults are present. Remember that good manners are intended to make those around us feel comfortable. Listening to an adult reprimand his or her child in an angry tone of voice is decidedly discomforting, so don't do it. If your child needs a reminder, take her aside or whisper in her ear. If you've been successful at making a project of learning the manner in question, whispering will do the trick.

5. Remember to praise. In giving praise, the most sincere expression is low-key and matter-of-fact. You don't need to jump up and down and clap your hands when your child does something right. A simple acknowledgment, as in "You did a good job with your manners tonight, and we're very proud of you" will suffice.

The following testimonial from a mother of three embodies this Five-Point Plan (she didn't know about it when she wrote me), so I pass it along in the hope that more parents will take up the cause.

"Before I had children of my own," said mother writes,

I could never understand why certain parents allowed their children to freely interrupt adults who were talking to one another, whether on the phone or person-to-person. My sister-in-law, for example: When I'm on the phone with her, she repeatedly stops talking to me and begins talking to her now seven-year-old son! I feel like I'm being abruptly put on hold every two minutes or so. I also have a friend who can't seem to figure out who she's talking to when I'm over at her house—me or her six-year-old daughter.

With my own children, I made sure this would not be a problem. Since none of them interrupt, I thought you might be interested. Here's my method:

When the child is two years old or, in some cases, even younger, I begin staging pretend practice sessions. I pretend to be talking to another adult, and the child pretends that he or she wants to ask me for a glass of water.

While I am "talking" to my imaginary friend, I have the child walk into the room and stand in a certain area. I'm very specific about where he should stand (about eight feet away). I tell him that he is to stand quietly until I recognize him, at which point I turn and ask, "Can I help you?" At that point, he is to say "Excuse me" before making his request. [Notice, folks, this mom teaches that "excuse me" is not used for the purpose of interrupting but is reserved for after one has been recognized.]

We do this a few times, and each time I tell him what a good job he did waiting for Mommy to finish talking, that it took a lot of patience to wait that long, and that he is very grown-up and has good manners. We hold practice sessions of this sort every day for a week, and each time I wait just a bit longer before I recognize the child. At the end of the week, a two-year-old is able to wait almost a minute!

After this, if the child forgets and interrupts an adult conversation, I have no trouble turning to him and saying, with a stern tone and an equally stern look, "You do not interrupt, and you know it." Typically, that jolts him into silence, and he waits while I continue my conversation. After a minute or so, I turn and ask, "Now, can I help you?" Sometimes, however, I don't have to, because the child has forgotten what he wanted and left the room.

If interrupting does occur, we hold another practice session later. I've never had to punish any of my kids for interrupting, as it has only hap-

pened once or twice with each, and my response was enough for them to remember next time that it is not allowed.

You should do a column on kids touching things in stores. I actually had a mother recently tell me that it's important not to discipline your child for touching things in stores. Her reasoning was that the children who have a strong desire to touch and feel things are very creative people, and if you deny them the privilege of touching everything they want in the store, then you are stifling their creativity.

All I can say is that my kids are very creative, but they don't touch things in stores.

It's encouraging to know there are parents who realize that the best discipline is preventive, because it hampers misbehavior and averts punitive discipline, and who don't use psychobabble as an excuse for misbehavior.

Like Rabbi Schneerson, William of Wykeham (1324–1404), the founder of both Winchester College and New College, Oxford, thought manners were so important to education that he coined "Manners maketh man" as the motto for both of these venerable institutions. Indeed, it is the grace of good manners, not soccer, piano, or gymnastics, not even good grades, that separates the men from the boys and the women from the girls. If you want your children to grow up graceful and charming and all those mannerly things that "maketh" maturity, put the majority of your parenting eggs in the basket that will ultimately count for more than any other that your children will carry with them into adulthood—the good manners basket!

Moral Education

I cannot leave a discussion of manners without emphasizing the importance of teaching religious values—otherwise known as morals—to children. Parents, take your children to church or synagogue or mosque. And if you get them involved in but *one* after-school activity, make it a religious youth group run by a competent young man or woman or a married couple who are themselves a model of marital devotion. All of the research clearly indicates that children who attend a church, regardless of denomination, children who acquire a solid grounding in moral values through ongoing moral instruction, are far, far, *far* less likely to engage in antisocial and/or self-destructive behavior of any kind, especially through their critical teen years. They are less likely to use drugs, have premarital sex, be arrested for any reason, or develop behavior or academic problems, and far more likely, as adults, to enter into marriages that succeed.

This has been confirmed over and over again in research done by the National Institute of Healthcare Research, the Heritage Foundation, the University of Nebraska and Arizona State University West, and the National Longitudinal Study on Adolescent Health (LSAH), and through the National Center on Addiction and Substance Abuse (CASA) at Columbia University. Here's what LSAH researcher Michael Resnick wrote in the *Journal of the American Medical Association* in 1997:

> *Social science has also begun to suggest that religion, a subject that social scientists are notoriously reluctant to touch, has a significant effect, independent of economic status, in keeping children out of trouble. Evidence has begun to accumulate that in the inner city, church-going males are less likely to commit crimes than are others of the same economic status. There is evidence, suggestive though not yet conclusive, that religious programs in prison reduce criminal recidivism for prison inmates more than what one would find among similar inmates in the same prison. We do not know whether fostering religion in a child or supporting the youth-saving work of churches will produce the same effects that we now observe in the simple connection between religiosity and decency. But religiosity and decency are correlated; in time, we may learn that the former causes the latter.*

Joseph Califano was secretary of health, education, and welfare during Jimmy Carter's presidency. He subsequently chaired the CASA project. Speaking not just to the importance of religion in a child's life, he reinforces, by implication, what I've said about the relative unimportance of after-school activities.

Religion is a key factor in giving our children the moral values, skill and will to say "no" to illegal drugs, alcohol and cigarettes.... If parents take their children to religious services beginning at a very early age they can have a major impact on whether or not their children resist these substances.... Parental involvement is a critical protective factor. The more often teens eat dinner with their parents, the less likely they are to smoke, drink or use marijuana.

Every successful culture has been built upon a strong foundation of religious values, and every culture, in its decline, has abandoned religious values and replaced them with secular ones. Religious values provide a child with guideposts for living a good and righteous life, not to mention the strength to "just say no" to a myriad of temptations, including the need to resolve conflict by resorting to violence.

It has long been my contention that children who grew up in the 1950s and 1960s were much better behaved than are today's kids. Don't misunderstand me. We were far from perfect. We misbehaved, of course, but most of the bad stuff we did was nothing more than mischievous, especially when compared with what kids are doing today. In this regard, it is significant to note that the teen crime rate, across the socioeconomic spectrum, has soared since the 1960s and that today's teen criminals are committing what were once considered adults-only crimes: rape, murder, assault with a deadly weapon, armed robbery, drug peddling.

In my day, kids were mischievous and covert. We tried to get away with misbehavior when adults weren't looking and, we hoped, wouldn't find out. School administrators and teachers tell me that today's kids don't seem to care if they're caught. I'm told this is because they have no fear of adults or consequences. I suppose this is because adults no longer give children reason to fear them or what they might do.

We also knew when we had misbehaved. Take cheating, for example. In 1965, the year I graduated from high school, if a kid cheated on a test, he knew what he had done was wrong, wrong, wrong. If caught, he wouldn't have said to the teacher, "Hey! I cheat because that's what you have to do if you want to get into a good college."

Believe it or not, that's what today's kids often say when they're caught cheating. A recent study conducted by Donald McCabe, the founding president of the Center for Academic Integrity at Rutgers University, found that almost three out of four high school students from around the USA report having cheated on a major test or written work (i.e., plagiarism). McCabe found, furthermore, that few of these kids have any shame or regret. "You do what it takes to succeed in life," wrote one cheater. Another, who plagiarized several sources for a paper on *Macbeth*, said, "Remorse just slows you down." That's more than a bit scary.

Today's cheaters also note that when others are caught, nothing of consequence happens to them. When I was in school, if you cheated in a class, you probably flunked it (and your parents would not have hired a lawyer to defend your "rights"). If you cheated on a final exam, you might have been expelled. Today, kids who cheat are often simply made to take another form of the test, or rewrite the plagiarized paper. The worst that usually happens to a student who cheats is that he or she receives a zero on the assignment in question.

I didn't cheat because I was afraid—petrified is more like it—of what would happen if I was caught. Today, what's to fear? In fact, a teacher who has the nerve to give a cheater a failing grade might wind up in trouble. That's what actually happened in Kansas during the school year 2001–02. When a high school English teacher failed nearly two dozen students for plagiarizing from the Internet, their parents complained, the superintendent forced the teacher to give the kids good grades, and she resigned.

You see, the problem really isn't kids. Kids have always tried to get away with what they could. The problem is adults who avoid saying that cheating is just plain wrong, that there is no excuse for it. For example, in a *Washington Post* article on cheating, a reporter wrote that today's students "haven't become moral reprobates in a generation" (i.e., they aren't to blame); rather, the problem is that the Internet makes it too easy to cheat. "Who could resist?" she concludes.

That's insane. The fact is, one out of four students resists, proving that the problem is not the Internet. The problem is that today (a) a lot of kids are moral reprobates who think, as do all criminals, that the end justifies the means; and (b) a lot of adults are just too darned chicken to stand up to America's epidemic of kid crime.

Questions?

Q: *My very social, outgoing five-year-old daughter has recently started addressing adults with "Yo, dude!" She picked this up from an older sister who jokingly uses this talk with her around the house (but never with adults). I think this behavior is obnoxious and have explained the difference between a proper greeting and an improper one. The problem is that she's confused about being punished for this because most adults seem to take it with a grain of salt and get a good laugh out of it! When I correct her in front of one of these adults, the adult is likely to say, "Oh, don't be silly. She's so cute and funny." I don't think it's funny. I think it's rude and disrespectful. I'm at a loss for a polite comeback to get these folks to understand I'm trying to raise a daughter with good manners.*

A: The appropriate comeback is "Look, if you can't support me here, then keep your big fat mouth shut, dude!"

I'm only kidding, of course. Actually, you know I agree with you. However, I have to tell you that unless your daughter cannot understand simple concepts, which I'm sure is not the case, she is not confused. You've explained your expectations properly, and she's smart enough to understand. The laughs she's getting from adults simply overwhelm any punishment you can dole out. You need to accept that, but you need to continue punishing her for her disobedience. You would also do well to tell her older sister that she is no longer allowed to say "Yo, dude!" even jokingly around the house.

Better yet, bring your five-year-old daughter to my house and introduce her to me. When she calls me a "dude," I'll give her a withering look and say, "Excuse me? I'm not a dude, certainly not to a five-year-old. I'm Mr. Rosemond, thank you." That'll make her think twice about ever again calling an adult a dude. Come to think of it, find someone in your own hometown who will say that to her. Set it up. If the first time doesn't work, set it up again with someone else who's willing to help you. In the final analysis, that will be a lot more effective than punishing her.

Q: *My daughter is six years old, and I am concerned because she rarely makes eye contact when speaking to anyone. Stacy is very bright, listens well, makes friends easily, will answer questions in class, and even likes to give reports or share with the entire class. Her karate instructor first pointed out that she did not make eye contact when she was five years old and even suggested to me that she might have attention deficit disorder. Her pediatrician and kindergarten teacher said that was ridiculous. Ever since then, I have tried to make eye contact with her when I speak, but I don't see it getting better. Her two-year-old sister looks me right in the eye when she speaks to me, which makes Stacy's lack of eye contact that much more glaring to me. Do I need to be concerned about this, and if so, how can I encourage eye contact without being draconian?*

A: Lack of eye contact is sometimes symptomatic of developmental problems, but not when the child in question is otherwise social, communicative, and well-behaved. One isolated odd behavior is not generally sig-nificant of anything other than the fact that (if the truth were known) we all have our oddities.

I recommend that you deal with this head-on and with a fairly strict approach. In other words, I don't think you're going to get very far trying to encourage eye contact. And as far as being draconian, well, if by that you mean strict, I think strict is what's necessary. Today's parents want to discipline misbehavior without causing their children discomfort. That's a nice idea, and there are even some professionals who maintain that it's possible. Personally, I think it's a pipe dream.

First, in a child of this age, not giving eye contact to an adult who is speaking to you is clearly misbehavior—at age three, no; but at age six, yes. Second, a misbehaving child cannot be talked into behaving prop-erly. You need to tell your daughter, in no uncertain terms, that not looking at people when they talk to you is rude, no less rude than not acknowledging that someone has said "hello" to you. It's a matter of good manners, and you will no longer tolerate her behaving in this fashion toward other people, including yourself.

For two weeks, help her acquire the habit of maintaining eye contact with people through role play. When she does the right thing, praise her; when her eyes wander, stop her and get her to look at you. After this initial transitional period, begin the project: Allow her two "no eye contact" violations—or freebies—a day. The third violation results in suspension of special privileges for the rest of the day and early bedtime. When she's operating successfully within this quota, reduce her daily "freebie" to one. With consistency, you ought to see significant improve-ment in a few weeks, if not sooner. Just remember, Rome wasn't built in a day. What has taken seven years to develop, however, can be set on the right road in a relatively short period of time if you're willing to be a bit more draconian than you'd like to be.

Q: *We have two children, ages eight and seven. The older is severely handicapped. Ever since her younger brother realized the nature and extent of her mental and physical disabilities, he has gone through periods of resentment toward her for commanding so much of our attention. Repeated explanations of why things are that way seem to fall on deaf ears. His most common complaint is that it isn't "fair" that she's his sister. These episodes last for a couple of weeks, and then, as quickly as he started complaining, he'll stop, only to start back up again within a couple of months. We try to spend as much individual time with him as we can, but nothing seems to satisfy. To give him any more attention, we would have to place our daughter in a residential facility, which is not an option. What can we do?*

A: You have obviously never heard of Rosemond's Blue in the Face Principle: One's face begins turning blue the second time one explains the same concept or idea to a child.

How blue must your face become before you realize that you are not going to put an end to your son's complaining by patiently explaining his sister's condition to him? If he is intelligent, and there is nothing you have not said concerning his sister's need for nearly constant attention, then it's time to stop explaining and tell him to get a grip. You need to put an end to this soap opera before it turns your son into an incurable kvetch.

The next time he complains about the unfairness of his miserable life, I would recommend a conversation along these lines: "You ought to be ashamed for thinking so much about yourself. If anyone has a right to complain about life being unfair, it's your poor sister. Why, you'll be able to move away from her problems in about eleven years, but *she* will never be able to get away from them. There is only one explanation for your complaints, which is that we have spoiled you rotten. So we've decided that, from now on, every time you complain about your sister, you are going to give a favorite toy to charity. We're putting a charity box in the back hall. When it's full, we'll take it to a charity that will give your things to children who appreciate what they have. And we will never, ever talk about your unfair life again. Enough is enough. Any questions?"

Whatever a child practices often, he will become good at. If you want a child to become a good, even great, golfer, start him young and have him practice often. If you want a child to become a chronic, world-class grumbler, let him get started when he is young and allow him the freedom to practice often. In other words, the longer you wait to put a heavy lid on your son's complaining, the more likely it is that whining and moaning will forever dominate his personality.

Your son is growing up in circumstances that are not ideal, for sure, but he has no idea how good his life truly is when compared with the lives of more than half the world's children, not to mention the life of a sister who lacks even the ability to know how bad the quality of her life is. No, your son does not need more attention. He needs a major attitude adjustment.

Q: *We recently found pornographic material under our sixteen-year-old son's bed. Last year he battled depression, bad grades, and drug use, but this year he's made a big turnaround. He's upbeat, has a job, is making good grades, and goes to church. But just when we thought we were out of the woods, this pornography thing comes along. My husband says that I shouldn't have been searching his room and that for a sixteen-year-old boy to be looking at such material is perfectly normal; he thinks we should ignore the matter. I'm not entirely comfortable with that. Then again, if we raise the issue, I'm going to have to explain why I was snooping. What do you think?*

A: First, I agree that this is a delicate matter. On the one hand, it's reasonable for parents to do an occasional sweep of a teenager's room when the child in question has a history of drug use, even if there are no tangible signs of relapse. But justifying such a search requires some reason other than mere parental curiosity. Legitimate reasons would include sudden changes for the worse in mood, behavior, social life, or school grades. Given your son's complete turnaround and the absence of such indicators, I do not feel that a search of his room, at this time, was appropriate. Furthermore, I think letting him know you conducted a search might cause a setback in your relationship, something you should be trying to avoid.

On the other hand, possession of pornography by a sixteen-year-old boy is not something that should be ignored. True, as your husband states, it is normal for teenage boys to be attracted to sexual material. That does not make it healthy. Pornography is potentially addictive and is associated not only with inappropriate sexual attitudes but also with deviant and sometimes even antisocial sexual behavior. For example, nearly all child molesters have a history of high involvement with pornography. Heterosexual pornography depersonalizes women, reducing them to sexual objects, because the underlying message is that it's perfectly okay to view and even use them as such. This is not to say that any teenage boy who looks at pornography on a regular basis is going to grow up with a distorted sexual ethic or engage in inappropriate sexual activities, but the risk is there.

One way to deal with this sort of thing is simply to make the inappropriate material disappear from your son's room. Say nothing. He will get the message and at the very least will stop bringing such material into your home. He might even take his dad aside and want to talk about it, which would open the door for a creative conversation. If you decide to go with this option, Dad should be prepared for the talk. In other words, he should figure out what he wants to get across and have his "tape" ready to roll. This will, of course, require an explanation as to how the material was discovered, in which case Dad should come up with something other than "Mom was snooping."

A friend of mine, when he discovered a *Playboy* magazine in his son's room, just left it on the bed. He said nothing about it, mind you. Two days later his son came to him and confessed that he couldn't stand the silence and wanted to talk, at which point the two of them had one of the best conversations they'd ever had.

A young man's dad is the ideal person to deal with an issue of this sort. Your husband might be persuaded simply to take your son aside and, without any reference to the contraband, open the door to a discussion about mature, respectful attitudes toward women. In the course of this discussion, he can simply bring up the subject of pornography as an example of disrespect toward women and also oneself. Assuming your son and his father have a good relationship, this message should have a very positive impact.

5

Fundamental Parenting Principle Five

It's About Responsibility, Not High Achievement

> *Even a child is known by his actions;*
> *by whether his conduct is pure and right.*
>
> —Proverbs 20:11

To be a responsible person means three things: (1) to carry out assignments from legitimate authority figures to the best of one's ability; (2) to be willing to give necessary assistance to others or do what needs to be done without being asked or told; and (3) to accept full responsibility for the consequences of one's own behavior, which is also known as *accountability*. The presence of these three qualities in a person's character constitutes the fullness of good citizenship, and as Grandma said, "Good citizenship begins in the home."

The first two aspects of responsibility are the essence of what is known as a *work ethic*. They are instilled in a child through the assignment of household tasks. By doing chores, by contributing to the maintenance of the family's environment, a child is initiated into full membership in the family. She takes on a meaningful role in the group and becomes a full participant. Chores teach the child that citizenship carries obligations as well as confers privilege, that privilege and obligation go hand in hand, and that the former is the fruit of the latter. For this reason, a child should not be paid for performing chores on behalf of the family. Payment obscures the fact that chores are an obligation, a contribution to the welfare of the family as a whole. Indeed, it should be made clear to a child from the first assignment of a regular routine of daily chores (which should occur, ideally, shortly after the child's third birthday) that her privileges depend upon the proper discharge of her obligations to the family. In short, if she fails to do her chores, her privileges will be withheld.

I am a member of the last generation of American children to be raised according to the precepts of this citizenship ethic. Most people who were raised in the 1950s and 1960s will attest to having had daily chores from an early age, chores for which we were not paid. We did them because we were told to do them, period. We had to finish our chores, and satis-factorily, before we could go outside and play. In other words, we had to do what we *had* to do (obligation) before we could do what we *wanted* to do (privilege). Nearly everyone in my generation remembers calling on a friend only to have his mother tell you that he couldn't come outside until he'd finished doing his chores. This didn't happen every once in a while, mind you; it happened with regularity, several times a month. Eventually, you learned when your friend could come outside and when he couldn't because his chores, as did yours, occurred at predictable times—they were part of his daily routine.

Unfortunately, as the emphasis in child rearing has shifted from that of producing a good citizen (the child's parents' obligation to the culture) to instilling high self-esteem, parents have stopped assigning chores. Today, it is rare to find a child who is a good citizen of his or her family, who has a meaningful role within his or her family, who is a contributor to the family as well as a consumer of the family's "fruits." All too often, the only people in the modern family who act as if they have obligation are parents, and they mostly feel that their duties are to their children, whom they put at the center of attention and treat like little royalty. In the all-too-typical contemporary American family, the parents serve the children, and the children perform no service whatsoever. In effect, the children are on a perpetual entitlement program; they enjoy privilege without obligation.

The mother of a four-year-old recently told me proudly that her child had a chore.

"A chore?" I inquired.

"Yes," she said. "Her chore is to let me know when the dog's bowl needs to be filled."

I was close to dumbstruck. "And who fills the bowl when it needs filling?"

"Why, I do," the mother replied. "If I let her do it, she puts too much food in the bowl and spills water on the floor."

In other words, the child tells the mother when the mother needs to perform a chore. If this wasn't so absurdly pathetic, it would be funny, but the truly sad thing is that the mother in question doesn't even realize that this supposed chore does nothing but give this child opportunity to exercise authority over her mother. As for putting too much food in the bowl and spilling water, those are not reasons for not letting a child perform a task; rather, they are reasons for teaching the child how to measure out the right amount of food and use a sponge to mop up spills. But such is the sorry state of parenting in twenty-first-century America.

In the course of a presentation to an assemblage of parents, I sometimes say, "You all seem to think your children are gifted, but you often treat them as if they were idiots."

This never fails to bring a big laugh as the audience members realize the contradiction between what they believe their children are capable of (anything) and what they expect them to do (next to nothing). I then point out that to truly *respect* a child means to *expect* of the child.

"Unfortunately," I say, "many of you gathered here today expect very little of your kids. You expect a lot of yourselves. You expect so much of yourselves, in fact, that your children begin expecting a lot from you as well. This is how a child becomes demanding, petulant, and ungrateful, and begins to act put upon any time you ask anything of him.

"Raise your hand if that describes your child," I ask.

It never fails: More hands go up than not.

Before I was four years old, my mother, a working single parent at the time, taught me how to wash floors, and from that time on, I washed our floors on a regular basis. Before I was five years old, Mom taught me to wash my own clothes in her "washing machine," which consisted of a galvanized tub with hand rollers bolted to it that sat on the side porch.

Lots of kids lived in my neighborhood. Every single one of us, by age four, had daily chores that had to be done before we could go outside and play. This was the early 1950s, when parents expected children, even very young children, to perform household tasks, thus demonstrating their respect for their children. Parents of that day were unlikely to give two seconds of thought to their children's IQ. Parents didn't brag about their children back then, much less drive around town with signs on their cars proclaiming that their children were a cut above in the intellect department. But every parent back then knew that a child, regardless of how smart, was a *capable, competent* human being, and the parent was not going to let that competence atrophy from disuse.

A mother recently asked me, "John, I know you believe children should have chores before they are four. My daughter will be four in a few months. What chores can I reasonably expect her to do at this age?"

"Teach her to wash floors," I replied.

She looked at me like I'd said something unintelligible. "You must have misunderstood me, John," she said. "My daughter's not even four yet."

"No, I heard you correctly. She's old enough to learn to wash floors. You should teach her to wash a small area first, like the bathroom floor, and when she's mastered that, move her to bigger and bigger spaces."

She gave me another incredulous look. "Um, I really think she's a bit young for that."

This mom probably tells people she thinks her daughter is gifted but then treats her daughter as if she is not capable of learning something as simple as washing a floor. The importance of learning to wash a floor to this or any child is not in learning to perform the task itself; rather, it is in learning that she is a capable, competent, trustworthy person. It is in knowing that she has a part in keeping the home clean and comfortable. It is in knowing that she is making a valuable contribution to the family's day-to-day welfare.

I doubt that the mother in question went home and taught her daughter how to wash floors or any equivalent task, in which case this supposedly gifted child is still being treated as if she's incompetent. This mother, like many American parents, probably brags about her daughter but doesn't really respect her because, remember, to truly *respect* a child means to *expect* of the child. Unfortunately, the girl in question, like all too many of today's kids, is probably going to be on an entitlement program for her entire childhood. She's going to be on what I call "family welfare," never learning that citizenship, the relationship between the individual and society, is a give-and-take proposition; never learning that the success of any relationship depends on giving as much as one gets.

The consequences of this nouveau child-rearing philosophy and style are already being felt in our culture as children raised within its weaknesses grow up and enter the workplace. Time and time again, employers and managers have complained to me about the fact that so many young people lack a responsible work ethic. They want from their employers but are unwilling to give in kind. They bring to the workplace a set of expectations learned in their families: that the employer has obligations to them but they have few obligations in return. They expect from their employers what their parents taught them to expect at home: entitlement.

A younger friend of mine is a manager at one of this country's largest banks. He recently told me that he gently confronted a young employee for making mistakes that were costly in both time and money. He encouraged him to be more careful in the future. The employee, in his early twenties, responded that it wasn't his responsibility to catch his own mistakes.

"Whose responsibility is it then?" my friend asked.

"I don't know, but it's not mine. You figure it out."

"Excuse me," my friend responded. "But it's your job; therefore, it's your responsibility."

At this point, the young man looked at an equally young co-worker and said, "I can't deal with this anymore. You explain it to him." And walked away!

I'll just bet that when this young person was in elementary school, his parents took on the responsibility of checking his homework for mistakes and then helped him correct them. I'll just bet that this young person was choreless for eighteen years. I'll just bet that this young person, like so many kids of his generation, enjoyed the fruits of family welfare for as long as he lived in his parents' house. I'll just bet that his parents felt it was their job to protect him from negative consequences (to guard his holy self-esteem, of course).

The consequences of raising children in this weak and weakening fashion, multiplied by millions, will have an eventual devastating effect on the strength of democracy in America, on the American economy, and on our sustainability of marriage. As a culture, we are already in the early stages of that devastation.

My question to you, the reader, is this: Are you going to be part of the problem, or are you willing to become part of the solution? This situation has not gone past the tipping point where it cannot be solved. Will you do your part to stop America from sliding into a moral abyss?

Accountability

A mom recently told me that when her daughter had been passed over for captain of the cheerleading squad for a girl with less seniority, she had gone to the school and confronted the squad's coach, demanding a reassessment.

"A parent should stand up for a child when a teacher is treating the child unfairly, right?" she asked, rhetorically.

"I'd stay out of it," I replied, at which point the esteem in which I had been held just moments before fell like the stock market on Black Friday.

My parents would have stayed out of such things, and there were certainly times when teachers treated me with less than complete fairness. In my parents' view, shared by most of their premodern peers, the world was not a fair place, and the sooner a child came to grips with that reality, the better for the child and all concerned. Let's face it, folks, it is inconceivable that a child will be treated fairly at all times by all teachers through thirteen years of school.

"But," a reader might protest, "in a conflict with a teacher, a child automatically loses. Someone needs to balance the teacher's authority."

Let's back up. First, "fair" is in the eye of the beholder. Therefore, it is not possible for anyone to exercise legitimate authority and have her decisions always perceived as "fair" by everyone. The fact that a student and her parents feel a teacher acted unfairly does not mean the teacher acted illegitimately. In this Age of Entitlement, Americans seem to be forgetting the difference between a politician and a leader. To be effective, a leader must make unpopular decisions. A politician tries to make popular decisions, which is why most politicians are not good leaders. A teacher is not a politician. She is a leader of children. I say this knowing full well that many of today's teachers, like many parents, are trying to be popular with children, thus neutralizing their authority. The fact that most adults do not claim their legitimate authority over children has led to the ubiquitous feeling that adult authority figures should treat children fairly. In short, today's teachers are rapidly becoming their own worst enemies.

When my daughter, Amy, was in junior high school, she began complaining of a teacher who had favorites, and she was not one. She felt this was unfair, but she was not referring to the teacher's attempt to be friends with certain students. She was angry because she was not one of his "picks." I listened to Amy complain about this teacher on a nearly daily basis, simply saying things like "That's too bad" and "This too will pass," which upset her even more.

Finally, the teacher called me to complain about Amy's attitude. I told him I wanted to support his authority, but he was his own worst enemy. By playing favorites, he was fostering jealousies that undermined his students' ability to see him as an authority figure. How, I asked, could I effectively support something he was not effectively exercising? Our conversation ended with him thanking me for my remarks.

The desire to be treated fairly is tantamount to the belief that one is generally entitled to never be treated other than how one wants to be treated. In other words, people who believe they should be treated fairly are children, no matter their actual ages, and there is no one more obnoxious than a child who looks like a fully grown-up person. As for teachers treating children fairly, if this means giving them the grades they deserve, fine. If it means punishing them for their misdeeds, fine. If it means, however, that teachers should not upset students, not fine at all. Unfortunately, when it comes to how other adult authority figures treat their Most Preciousnesses, many parents define "fair" in the latter sense.

I remember when I was in junior high school, there were a couple of bratty kids who were small for their age but formed protection pacts with bullies. The brats would help the bullies with their homework; in return, the bullies would protect the brats from retaliation when they acted like brats. The brats, therefore, were free to act as provocatively as they wished. They'd hit other kids from behind, knock their books out of their hands, mess up their carefully coiffed hair, and constantly taunt them, calling them all manner of humiliating names. The kids couldn't do anything about it, of course, because if they tried to defend themselves from the brats' assaults, the bullies would step in and cause memorable pain.

From what I'm hearing around the country, similar pacts are common-place today. It seems that quite a number of kids have their own personal bullies protecting them from consequences of any sort when it comes to bratty, provocative, and/or irresponsible behavior. These bullies are their parents.

In a major southeastern city, two high school football standouts stole a vehicle and took it for a joyride, after which they dumped it in a river. The principal tossed the kids off the team. The parents of both boys countered with lawsuits, claiming that the principal's ruling "ruins the boys' chances of securing college football scholarships." The boys didn't ruin their own chances; rather, Principal Meanie tried to do so. Suddenly, the little criminals are victims and the legitimate authority figure is the villain.

In 2003, a teacher at a midwestern elementary school refused to change a child's grade. Privately, the child's father threatened the teacher with physical punishments of various diabolical sorts if he did not consent to the parents' demands. The principal felt the threats were serious enough to warrant additional security personnel at the school, part of whose job it was to escort the teacher to and from his car.

It would seem that I am describing people who qualify as low-life, brutish, uncultured, ignorant slobs. Not so. The parents in both examples are well-to-do folks who live in expensive houses and drive expensive cars. In fact, from what I observe, many of these incidents involve parents whose social standing is inconsistent with such loutish behavior. Nonetheless, they are bullies. If they don't physically threaten someone who "abuses" one of their precious children by giving out a "wrong" grade, disciplining "unfairly," or making a bad call during a game, they threaten lawsuits.

An independent school head recently remarked, "Our problems are not so much with students as with parents." She echoed similar comments from countless other school administrators and teachers across the USA. Forty years ago, it was the rare parent who did not support discipline meted out at school. Today, it is the rare parent who does. The proliferation of parent-child protection pacts has resulted in an epidemic of children who have license to act as provocatively as they please.

As a principal recently told me, "Invariably, the very kid with parents who threaten a lawsuit when he's disciplined is one of the worst behaved children in the class, if not the whole school."

The reader has every right to ask, "So, John, what's the solution?"

The solution is for these parents to change their way of thinking about their children and their responsibilities toward them, which in my own small way, I seek to help them do through the vehicle of this book.

Excuses, Excuses

When I misbehaved, and it didn't matter whether the misbehavior occurred at home, school, or in the neighborhood, my parents rarely asked me to explain myself. In fact, if I even tried to propose an explanation, they would generally cut me off by saying something along the lines of "There are no excuses." As I now realize, every prospective explanation was an attempt to excuse myself, to justify what I had done, to pass the buck, to turn wrong into less than wrong, if not right. Children have been doing this since Day One. Read Western civilization's first parenting story, Genesis, chapter 3, and note that Adam passed the buck to Eve, and Eve passed it on to the serpent. They were not willing to accept responsibility for what they had done in full knowledge that it was wrong. That's kids for you.

When their children misbehaved, Tom Brokaw's "Greatest Generation" acted. In the 1960s, however, parents began listening to experts who promoted the notion that good parenting was primarily a matter of how well one talked to one's child. So, where yesterday's parent acted, today's parent tends to talk, and not just talk, but talk talk talk talk talk talk and then talk some more. Talking is not all bad, but the time and place for it are not always and everywhere. Adding to the problem, in the course of all this talk talk talk, many of today's parents actually help their children evade responsibility for misbehavior.

A mother recently told me that her five-year-old is misbehaving at school. Nearly every day he brings home a bad behavior report, and she responds by sitting down and talking with him about it. What happened? she asks. Why did you do this and that? What were you feeling? Oh, and what did she do then? And how did you feel about that? And what did you do then? And why did you do that? And what might you have done instead? Mom told me she always feels these conversations help her son come to a "better understanding of how to act better next time," but when the next time happens, he acts badly again. Sometimes he acts even worse, in which case they talk some more.

Unwittingly, this mom is giving her son opportunity to construct excuses for his misbehavior, to explain it away. These Socratic exercises have taken the place of consequences. I propose that instead of leaving these conversations wanting to act better, he leaves them understanding that he can act pretty much any way he wants to because (a) nothing is going to happen of any consequence, just talk; and (b) he has his reasons, and if his reasons don't sound good to anyone else, they sure sound good to him. Besides, given his age, I bet he knows without being told that what he did was wrong and what he should have done instead.

The opportunity to construct excuses gives a child a chance to create, in his or her mind, a case for acquittal. If it's not accepted, then the problem lies not with the child, but with the adult, who simply doesn't understand. Just like that, the child is transformed in his or her own mind from someone who behaved badly into someone who is misunderstood.

When a child misbehaves, an adult needs to impress upon the child that when he or she makes a bad decision, bad consequences result. It is not bad to have your parent sit down and talk to you. It's simply inconvenient. It's bad to have your bicycle and television privileges taken away for a week, to have a weekend spend-the-night canceled, or to have to write a letter of apology to the offended party. Punishment is bad, and when dealing with bad behavior, one must fight fire with fire.

After a parent has punished, talk is fine, but first things first. Always take care that your talk does not open the door to excuses. Remember, there are none.

This problem—parents who believe their children are incapable of wrongdoing—has also been caused by postmodern psychological parenting. Before parents applied psychological explanations to their children's misbehavior, they thought about it in very dispassionate, objective terms. If a child told a lie, his parents said to themselves and each other, "Billy told us a lie," and Billy was punished. Now, however, if a child lies, his parents ask themselves, "Why did Billy feel that he had to lie?" Do you see the difference? Fifty years ago, it didn't matter why a child had lied. He had lied, period. In many cases, if he tried to offer up an explanation for his lying, his parents said, "There'll be no ifs, ands, or buts about this, young man, and if you open your mouth in your own defense, you'll be in twice as much trouble!" Why didn't they let him even explain himself? Because in the course of said explanation, he would have lied again. They were simply trying to avoid having to punish him twice.

My point is that today's parents are more interested in the why than they are in the behavior itself. These explanations are psychological; as in Billy has lied because he is afraid to tell the truth because he is afraid that his cold, distant father will further reject him if he admits to his wrongdoing, and furthermore, he is afraid of disappointing his very judgmental, puritanical mother. Or at least the parents fear that the *real* explanation (as opposed to Billy's) is something along these lines, and that it will indict them. So, in defending Billy, in denying that he did something wrong, in accusing a teacher of treating Billy unfairly in the first place, or whatever, they are actually defending themselves, keeping their worst fears at bay.

In generations past, if a child misbehaved in school, his teacher punished him. Then she might have sent him to the principal, who punished him again. The principal then called the child's home and spoke to his mother, who upon hearing the report, said, "Send him home. I'll take care of it." At home the child was punished by his mother. Then, when his father arrived home from work, he was punished again. Today, when a child misbehaves in school, and a teacher or principal calls the home, the parents—mother, most likely—begin acting as the child's advocates and attorneys. The mom denies that the teacher saw what she saw. She accuses the teacher of ignoring her child's special needs or of having a personality conflict with her child. Suddenly, the teacher is holding the hot potato. The parents might even threaten legal action, which upsets the principal. In the course of calming the parents down, he agrees with them that the teacher handled the situation badly. So you know what a lot of teachers do? They deal with classroom misbehavior as well as they can and never tell anyone except other teachers about it. Who can blame them?

Whose Homework Is It, Anyway?

Once upon a time not so long ago, homework was the bane of children's lives, and it belonged to the children alone. Today, it is the bane of not enough children and too many parents. When I was a schoolboy, the typical parent did no more than ask "Have you done your homework?" I remember my sixth-grade science teacher told the class that if he so much as suspected that a parent had helped with the annual science project, the student would receive an F, with no possibility of appeal. My good friend Charlie (and his dad) discovered the teacher was not bluffing. Today, the typical parent feels guilty if he or she is not helping with every assignment every night.

When I ask people my age why their parents never got involved in homework, the reply is always "I made sure my parents didn't get involved." When parents got involved in a child's homework back then, it was only because the child had not accepted his or her responsibility, and the consequence of parent involvement was usually punitive. In short, we did our homework because we were afraid not to. For those readers who are cringing at that, all of the available evidence indicates that the general mental health of children was much, much better in the 1950s than it is today. In other words, punishment was not bad for us; it was good for us.

Schools began encouraging parents to get involved with homework as the result of a 1970s study which found that, within a short time of arriving in the USA, Vietnamese children outperformed American students in science and math not because of superior ability but because their parents helped them with their homework. And not just parents but older siblings, grandparents, aunts, uncles, and cousins. Even neighbors would sometimes get involved in a child's homework assignment. Americans ignored the fact that in the Vietnamese family, homework was the medium for learning English as well as learning about American culture. The Vietnamese parents' attitude toward homework was taken out of its cultural context and promoted as the cure for the sinking achievement of all American children.

It turns out that parental involvement in homework has been a cure for nothing. Student achievement has continued to sink since the late 1960s. American students score near the bottom on international tests of science and math, and a recent study found that American children are abysmally ignorant of basic historical facts. The truth is that achievement levels were highest when American children did their own homework.

"But, John," not a few parents are countering, "if I left my child on his own to do homework, he simply wouldn't do it!"

That might be true, at least for a while. My usual professional experience has been that when parents pull out of the homework business, children do better in school. Maybe not right away, but eventually. Furthermore, one cannot simply hand responsibility for something to a child and then adopt a ho-hum attitude. The parent must be prepared to deliver appropriate motivation to the child if he or she fails to pick up the proverbial ball. There are children who have problems for which punishment is not appropriate, but personal and professional experience tells me that of all those who act like lazy good-for-nothings when it comes to homework, children with such problems are in the minority.

The bottom line: In most cases, children who are afraid of what will happen if they misbehave behave better than children with no such fear. The same applies to school performance, and I'm not just expressing opinion. Good research supports my position. The psychologist Diana Baumrind has conducted a three-decade study of the outcomes of various parenting styles. She has found that children whose parents love their children but punish them when they fail to toe the line behave better and have fewer problems in school than children whose parents try to reason bad behavior out of existence.

Don't misunderstand me. The child whose parents do not acknowledge and affirm good behavior and good school performance will not behave well and do well in school for long. For children to develop pride in their accomplishments, their parents must first be proud of them too.

Interest Versus Involvement

An outraged mother recently showed me a letter received from her son's second-grade teacher on the theme of parental involvement. Barely concealed between the lines, the message was "If you want good grades for your child, you'd best familiarize yourself with his assignments and sit with him while he does his homework."

"What do you think about stuff like this?" the mother asked.

I think it's outrageous. I think teachers ought to know better. A parent's regular participation in homework effectively prevents the child from assuming full responsibility for the work. It encourages dependency, short-circuits initiative, and denies the child the right to struggle with challenge. If grades are the issue, then parents who regularly participate in homework are helping in the short term only. If learning is the issue, then parents who regularly participate in homework are hurting their children in both the short and the long terms.

Parents should take keen interest in their children's education, but interest and involvement are horses of two different colors. To provide occasional guidance is fine, but to provide the steam that powers the homework engine is not. Unfortunately, the parent who refuses to become her child's nightly homework helper must accept that many of the other moms are dedicated to making sure their kids receive grades they do not deserve, grades that in most cases overstate ability. Thus, she must accept that her child may be one of the only ones in the class whose grades are an accurate reflection of his ability and his fortitude. Not an easy decision for a parent to make, but the right one, nonetheless.

For those parents who have the nerve to make it, I offer the following retort to the standard "Please be a good mom and help your child with his homework" letter:

Dear Teacher: With all due respect, I don't do my child's homework. I will not even always help her with it if she asks for help. Sometimes, I will simply tell her that she is smart enough to figure it out on her own. In any case, for me to figure it out for her is clearly not to her advantage. I am not a lazy parent, but I am not, and will not be, a micromanager either. Micromanagers do not bring out the best in people. They bring out the worst, regardless of whether they are known as "Boss" or as "Mom."

Keep sending the letters encouraging me to get involved in my child's homework, but I won't. Period. I'll provide necessary guidance, occasionally, and that's about it. One does not become a great pitcher if Mom is standing on the mound too, and one does not become a great student if Mom helps with homework every night, or even nearly so.

But here's my counteroffer. If my child does not do her homework or does not do the work she is capable of, let me know, and she will wish she had. Oh, fear not. I won't beat her or starve her, but I will surely teach her that irresponsibility results in undesirable consequences. Also, if she misbehaves in your class, just let me know, and I will teach her that misbehavior results in undesirable consequences. By the way, if her story concerning what happened is different from yours, I will believe you, even if I don't think you saw the big picture, in which case [child's name] will never know we had a difference of opinion. She also needs to learn that life isn't always fair, wouldn't you agree?

I hope this doesn't disappoint you greatly. I am actually your biggest supporter.

Questions?

Q: *My husband and I disagree over paying children for chores. He feels that just as we get compensated for doing our jobs, children should earn money for doing theirs. I say that their chores are a family obligation and that just as I don't get paid for cooking supper, they shouldn't be paid for feeding the dog and so on. Who's right?*

A: I agree with you that chores are obligations that should be shared among the members of a family according to age and ability. Applying the word *jobs* to a child's chores leads to the erroneous notion that they are in the same category as an adult's employment outside the home. The difference, of course, is that the parent's job provides for the child's standard of living. This creates an obligation that the child can discharge by performing chores. So the tasks are a service rendered to the family, a child's sole means of contributing to the general welfare. Furthermore, when the parent is at home, he or she has chores and family obligations for which he or she is not paid. Under the circumstances, paying a child to do what adults do simply because they must implies that children enjoy privileged status within the family, free from obligation, a dangerous notion indeed.

One would think that paying a child for doing chores is motivating. Not so. In fact, it has the opposite effect. Giving a child money for doing certain tasks creates the illusion that if the child doesn't feel the need for money at that point in time, he isn't obligated to do the chore. In this regard, I have never found a parent who pays for chores who does not have a difficult time getting the children to do them.

Paying for chores also obfuscates the fact that they are obligations. A chore that is paid for is no longer a contribution for the sake of the family but a service rendered for the sake of money. Paying for chores puts money in a child's pocket but no true sense of value in the child's head. It may teach something about business, but it teaches nothing whatsoever about the responsibility that accompanies family membership.

Although a family is not and should not be a democracy, chores can acquaint a child with the fact that the viability of a democracy such as ours depends on the ready willingness of the citizenry to lay down self-interests and render public service. The service ethic does not arise spontaneously; rather, it is learned. This is what Grandma was referring to when she said that good citizenship begins in the home.

Unfortunately, all too many of today's parents fail to give their children a regular routine of chores, as opposed to haphazard, unpredictable assignments. This failure contributes to the notion that the only persons with obligation in the parent-child relationship are the parents. Thus, they teach their kids that something can be had for nothing.

My standard recommendation is that a child should become acquainted with chores shortly after his or her third birthday. The chores should become part of the child's daily routine, as predictable as taking a bath before bedtime. Begin with tasks in the child's own sphere, such as picking up toys at a certain time every day. Build on the child's success by slowly expanding the responsibilities into the general sphere. It is not unreasonable to expect a five-year-old to contribute thirty minutes of work per day around the home. To anyone whose eyebrows are suddenly raised, let me point out that thirty minutes represents one-fifth the time the average five-year-old spends in front of a television set on a daily basis. Does the typical child have the time for chores? Of course! Like everything else, this is a simple matter of priorities.

Q: *Our twelve-year-old son and nine-year-old daughter share animal chores in the evenings. Every night we have to remind them, and they always put up a fight before the jobs get done. The tasks are definitely not too strenuous for them, and my husband and I feel the responsibility is good for them. What can we do to make sure they do their jobs, preferably without constant reminding and screaming (on their part, not ours)? The kids know that their chores need to be done every night and that they have to do them, yet they mess around until we start nagging, then they blow up. We are tired of all this. Help!*

A: I consulted the most recent edition of *Making Diagnostic Mountains Out of Molehills (MADMOM)*, indispensable to us mental health professionals, only to discover that your children are afflicted with both Explosive Reaction to Parental Pestering (ERPP) and Attention to Chores (ATCHOO) disorders, the first recorded cases of which appear in historical documents shortly after mankind's expulsion from the Garden of Eden, when chores became necessary.

The treatment plan is very specific: First, stop nagging and pestering. Tell the children something along these lines: "You will never, ever again hear either of us so much as refer to your chores. You know what they are, and we expect you to start them no later than (say) seven o'clock. If you have not started your chores by seven, we will do them for you. Sound good?" Say no more!

To any questions, reply, "That's really all we have to say." Then, just sit back and wait. The next time the kids let the designated start time lapse, just pick yourselves up, go outside, and start doing their chores. When you have finished, come inside and announce that it's time for them to go to bed. Be cheery! When they protest that bedtime is at least two hours away, say, "Oh, didn't we tell you? At seven o'clock, either you are on your way out the door to do your chores, or we are out the door to do them for you. If we do them, you have to go to bed as soon as we finish. In fact, if we put even one foot outside to do them, your opportunity has passed, so you might as well be in bed, lights out, by the time we come back. Oh, and by the way, if we do your chores on more than one night, Sunday through Friday, then all weekend privileges for you are canceled. Any questions?" All of this should be communicated in a matter-of-fact and therefore infuriating tone of voice, accompanied by dumb looks and many shrugs of your shoulders, as if to say, "Gosh, kids, we're real, real sorry about all this."

This will activate what I call the "Agony Principle": *Parents should not agonize over anything children do or fail to do if those children are perfectly capable of agonizing over it themselves.* The person or persons who become upset over a particular problem will try to solve it. In this case, you are trying to solve a problem—and driving yourselves slowly nuts in the process—that *only* your children can solve. They will solve it when you cause *them* to begin going nuts because of it.

Now, sit back, relax, and let them learn how the real world deals with people who do not accept their responsibilities. They're nine and twelve? Good, then it's not too late, but time's a-wastin'!

Q: *Two questions: In a recent column, you encouraged the practice of children doing chores and advised that parents not pay for this work. Are you also against allowances? Second, when two or more children are involved, should they alternate chores on some regular basis?*

A: I am not against giving a child an allowance as long as it has nothing to do with his or her chores. In other words, the allowance should not be used as a carrot to persuade the child to do chores, nor should it be withheld as punishment if the child fails to carry out responsibilities on time or properly. In this case at least, the left hand should not know what the right hand is doing.

Chores teach responsibility, self-discipline, time management, and numerous other life skills, all of which are essential to success in any adult endeavor. An allowance helps a child learn to manage money, but only if one condition is fulfilled: in giving the allowance, the parents also give the child responsibility for making purchases in a certain area. For example, the parents of a five-year-old might provide five dollars per week with which he is to purchase his own playthings. In this case, because the child's weekly allowance is insufficient for many of the things he wants, he is forced to learn to budget and save, of which any five-year-old is capable.

As for alternating chores between children on a regular basis, I recommend against it. Ask yourself, where in the real world does this happen? Does the person who is a teller at the bank one week become the president the next, only to be the janitor the next? The reader will immediately realize that this sort of arrangement would result in chaos. Likewise, confusion is the result of alternating chores between or among children.

Inevitably, the children argue over whose turn it is to do what chore. Because no task belongs exclusively to any one child, each takes less pride in doing it; therefore, they are likely to do just enough to get by. Then, when the parents point out that a certain task was not done properly, the children point their fingers at one another. Because the chores are alternated, it takes longer for any one child to learn to do any given chore efficiently. Alternating chores also prevents the children from falling into a routine. As a result of all this, parents find themselves constantly reminding and berating and hassling the children to get the tasks done. This is another example of how well-intentioned parental efforts to be fair often backfire.

"But, John," someone is saying, "if the children never alternate chores, then each of them learns only his or her chores and no one else's."

True. I'm referring, however, to alternating on a frequent basis. Exchanging tasks begins to make sense after each child in the family has adapted to the chore routine and become skilled at his or her responsibilities. This might take place every four months. The shorter the exchange interval, the higher the risk of the problems just enumerated.

A family is an organization—the most fundamental organizational unit in society, in fact. So everyone in it (except infants and young toddlers, of course) should pull together toward common goals, and everyone in the family should have the equivalent of a job description that helps define his or her role in the family and says, in effect, "You are a capable, competent person." This is a message to which most children will respond positively, if not at first then with encouragement and firm but patient direction and support.

Q: *Is it possible to get today's children to do their own homework? At the school our daughter attends, the teachers believe parents should orchestrate homework sessions—they call it "being a homework buddy." As a consequence, the children believe their parents should help them do their assignments. My husband and I, however, feel that children should do their homework independently. Mind you, we're willing to give help when it's truly needed, but we don't want to be our daughter's "buddies" under any circumstances. What are your thoughts on this?*

A: Yes, it is possible to get children to do their own homework, even in the face of teachers who want parents to be "homework buddies." The solution is very simple, actually, and since most of my parents' generation employed this very method, I can hardly claim copyright.

First, do not under any circumstances allow a child to do homework at the kitchen table or in any other family area. Make it clear that homework, being the child's work, is to be done in the child's room. Parents should make sure that the child has a well-lit desk and that his or her work area is stocked with appropriate supplies, such as paper, pencils and pens, crayons, a ruler, et cetera. Rule of Thumb: When homework is done in a family area, homework will become a family affair, thus diluting its benefit to the child in question.

Second, limit the number of times per evening you will render assistance to the child, and limit the length of any such help. For example, when our children were of school age, my wife and I made a rule that we would not provide help with more than three homework problems per evening, nor would any one helpful occasion exceed five minutes. Within these draconian limits, our children actually managed to make grades decent enough to get into good colleges.

I am convinced that one of the unintended messages the homework buddy system sends to children is that they are not competent. Therefore, it's not surprising that veteran teachers tell me today's kids act generally less capable than did children of twenty to thirty years past. Also, I have to think many a child has intuited that paying attention in class is less important than the degree of homework assistance his or her parents are going to render.

Third, hold children responsible for their school performance. Just as negative consequences befall irresponsible adults, negative consequences should befall children who do not accept their responsibilities. Lessons in real life should begin early, lest they come too late.

When all is said and done, the "I am not your homework buddy" system just described amounts to nothing more than proper discipline, which has always been the key to a child's success in school. Despite modern noises to the contrary, there is nothing new under the sun.

Q: *My second-grade son has received straight A's on both report cards this year. He receives only satisfactory marks in effort, however. His teacher recently sent a progress report in which she says he "often does not work to his potential." He often fails to read all of the directions on a work sheet and thus does not complete many assignments. This is compounded by the fact that he is usually*

in a hurry to finish his work and is careless. The teacher says he's very capable.
He reads with good comprehension, he can do math problems in his head, and
so on. His teacher says his problems boil down to a need to stay better focused.
Per your general advice, my son watches no television and has no video games.
He has chores, occupies himself well, and is well-behaved. What (if anything)
can I do to make him slow down with his work and read all directions?

A: This is prime example of the enabling that often substitutes for a tough-minded approach to children in today's schools, public and private. Here's a teacher who, instead of setting high expectations and enforcing them, lets a capable child slide, then raises red flags because the child has figured out that he is being given permission to slide.

The teacher is clearly saying that your son has sloppy work habits which result in incomplete assignments, yet she just as clearly does not penalize him for these problems. She gives him second chance after second chance to finish his work and correct his mistakes, then gives him straight A's! The fact that your son is not improving in his work habits is proof he is brilliant, a gifted child if ever there was one. He knows he doesn't have to change his ways in order to continue making good grades. It's quite simple, really: A child who does not work to his potential should not be receiving A's.

The teacher's statement that your son needs to be "better focused" is, of course, a way of hinting that he may have attention deficit disorder. Don't go there! This problem obviously does not reside within your son's nervous system, because he focuses quite well when he must. Rather, it is a function of this teacher's well-intentioned but dysfunctional approach to teaching. You need to confront her firmly but politely and inform her that you cannot motivate your son to be more conscientious concerning his work as long as she gives him A's for work that is substandard. She needs to penalize him for turning in assignments that are sloppy and incomplete. Furthermore, the grades she gives him should reflect his first attempt at an assignment, not his second or third. Tell her that you are perfectly willing to follow through with penalties at home for grades that are below par, but you simply cannot justify penalizing him for making the highest grades possible.

This is not education; it's coddling. And coddling does not bring out the best in a child. Rather, as this example shows, it brings out the worst.

Q: *Our sixteen-year-old daughter was struggling with algebra, so we got her a tutor. She has a part-time job. Do you think she should pay for all or part of the tutoring?*

A: The best approach to this issue that I've come across was submitted to my web site (www.rosemond.com). The parents in question required that the child (also a high school student with a part-time job) pay for her own tutoring, but if her grades improved, the parents reimbursed her. Needless to say, the child's grades improved. The principle is simple: One takes better care of that which is not free.

Q: *Our six-year-old constantly forgets things. He can't seem to remember things we tell him to do. In addition, he forgets to do his chores, give messages to people, and so on and on and on. We have started calling him Foggy because he seems to be in a fog nearly all the time. Mind you now, his teacher says it's not a problem at school, but it's constant at home. My husband says he had the same difficulty as a child, so we're wondering if it's inherited. In any case, can forgetfulness be cured, or are we just going to have to learn to live with it?*

A: No, forgetfulness is not inherited. More often than not, it's enabled, meaning the parents of "forgetful" children complain and wring their hands and implore the gods for relief but rarely put any real, consistent pressure on their kids to change their disobedient ways.

"Disobedient?" someone is exclaiming. "Oh, John, how can you be so insensitive? Forgetful and disobedient are two different things."

Not so. Note that the child in question usually forgets a responsibility, a task. I'll just bet he doesn't forget ice cream in the freezer or a promise his parents have made to him. No, like most children, he remembers what he wants to remember and forgets what he'd rather do without, like chores. This is a passive (and therefore less obvious) form of disobedience. Granted, the *rare* forgetful child may be so because of a *rare* learning disability, and I would not say that forgetfulness in a three-year-old is synonymous with disobedience, but in an otherwise able-minded six-year-old, constant forgetting is a form of disobedience and calls for discipline.

Here is the cure you requested: Make a list of your son's favorite privileges, such as riding his bike, having friends over to play, watching television, playing video games, and going to bed at his normal time. Post the list on the refrigerator, and every time he forgets to do something he's been told to do, cross off a privilege, beginning with his most favorite one. (If he loses his normal bedtime, he goes to bed an hour early.) Every privilege crossed off is lost until the following Monday. After you've tucked your son into bed on Sunday evening, wipe the slate clean by taking the previous week's list down and posting a new one in its place.

In the parlance of psychology, this is known as a "response-cost" system. In other words, your son's forgetful responses to instructions cost him things he values.

The yeast in this recipe is what I call the "Referee's Rule": No reminders, no warnings, no second chances. If he forgets, he loses a privilege. Bada bing, bada boom. I call this the Referee's Rule because you never see a referee give warnings or reminders. If he or she did, the game would deteriorate into chaos in a matter of minutes.

If you are consistent (i.e., dispassionate and ruthless) in applying this age-old method, I can virtually guarantee that over the next few months you'll witness an amazing improvement in your son's memory.

Q: *My husband and I have three boys, ages four, five, and eight. The two younger ones share a room that looks like Tornado Alley. They don't watch TV, so they color, play with Legos, tear up paper, and the like all day long. They give me no problem when I tell them it's time to clean up, but within minutes the room can look like a disaster zone again. The eight-year-old does the same thing but on a slightly smaller scale, since there's only one of him. I'm constantly telling them to straighten their rooms up and am beginning to feel like a certified nag. Should I just close the doors and let them have at it?*

A: You're not going to get a lot of sympathy from me or your fellow readers. After all, you've got three boys who (a) occupy their own time by playing creatively through the day, (b) clean up without complaint when you tell them to do so, and (c) are polite and respectful enough not to have told you that you are becoming a certified nag.

The source of your stress is not that your children make creative messes. After all, you should praise the Lord that they mess in their rooms and, in the meantime, leave you alone! Now you need to learn to leave them alone. One good turn deserves another, after all. No, the source of your stress is your own somewhat unreasonable expectation that they play creatively without making a mess. Let's face it, creative is messy.

Indeed, you should expect your sons to clean up their rooms, once a day, before bed. During the day, have them keep their doors closed. As they say, out of sight, out of mind.

Q: *Our thirteen-year-old son, an only child, is generally well-behaved and does well in school. This past summer, the three of us decided that William would begin working in his father's business one day per week during the summer and one weekend day during the school year to earn money and develop a good work ethic. We've had nothing but problems since. He claims that having to work is causing him to miss out on a social life and robbing him of a "fun" childhood. This is causing great conflict between him and his dad, and a lot of family problems overall. If William was your son, would you make him live up to the agreement?*

A: If making him live up to the agreement was going to create uproar in the family, I wouldn't. Upon discovering what he agreed to, if William wants to back out, I'd let him. At this age, trying to force compliance will succeed at the risk of precipitating great rebellion on his part. Besides, the fact that he doesn't want to work for his dad doesn't indicate he's going to be a lazy good-for-nothing when he grows up.

You asked what I would do if I was William's dad, so here goes: I would tell him he didn't have to work for me if he didn't want to. Under the circumstances, however, I would give him a weekly allowance of, say, twenty dollars (to a limit of eighty dollars per month). Thereafter, he would be responsible for purchasing his own nonessential clothing and recreation, unless the latter included other family members. Under no circumstances would I advance him money toward the next week's or month's allowance. If he felt he needed more money, he would have to ask me for work or ask neighbors if they have jobs for him. If he asked me for work and I found myself having to stand over him, however, I'd fire him, and that would be the end of it.

A management plan of this sort, which I've spelled out in great detail in my book *Teen-Proofing*, would force him to budget his money and begin confronting economic realities, including the "money doesn't grow on trees" principle. He would have a good measure of fiscal independence, he would learn by trial and error to make sound spending decisions, and the present tension in the father-son relationship would be defused.

I would also assign William at least one after-school or after-lunch chore per day (in addition to making his bed in the morning and keeping his room neat and clean), Monday through Saturday. His allowance and doing his chores would be completely independent of each other, however. In other words, he would do chores for free, simply because he is a member of the household. I wouldn't stand over him in this area either. If he doesn't do one of his chores, I wouldn't nag. I'd simply do it for him. But if I did one chore for him through the week, then his weekend privileges and freedoms would be revoked.

I don't believe in micromanaging a teenager or a child of any age, but a capable child should not be a freeloader, either. Do yourselves and William a favor and let him learn his life lessons the hard way. Stop trying to cram them down his throat.

Q: *My request for a certain third-grade teacher for my son was ignored by the principal. The teacher to whom he was assigned is very demanding, and that sort of approach just doesn't work with my son. The school year is not a month old, and an obvious personality conflict has developed between them. I've spoken to the principal, but she says my son is going to have to learn to take instructions from authority figures, whether he likes them or not. What can I do?*

A: I'll be blunt. It is simply not possible for a child to have a personality conflict with an adult who sits in a position of legitimate authority. Two adults can have a personality conflict. Two children can have a personality conflict. But a child and a teacher (or other adult authority figure) cannot. Period.

The idea that such a conflict might be possible is new, a function of the fact that the distinction between adult and child has blurred over the last forty or so years. In the 1960s, well-intentioned "experts" like the psychologist Thomas Gordon, author of *Parent Effectiveness Training,* promoted the idea that adult-child relationships should be democratic. Gordon and others who followed him wrote and spoke of the "democratic family" and the "democratic classroom." The implication behind these notions was that adults and children are equals, that they play on the same playing field. As this nefarious deconstructionist concept took hold in our culture, the idea that children are to obey adults mutated into the idea that adults are responsible for establishing a positive working relationship with children. In effect, this turns the adult-child relationship upside down. It puts adult authority figures in the position of trying to be liked by children, an effort that turns them into something other than people with authority.

Forty-six years ago, when I was eleven, I was expected to obey my teachers whether I liked them or not. I would not have dared tell my parents that a teacher didn't like me, because they would have immediately assumed I was doing something distinctly unlikable in the teacher's class, and they would have been right. Today, it is likely that a child who complains a teacher doesn't like him will be taken at his word, in which case the teacher may well wind up on the hot seat.

In the real world, an adult must obey legitimate authority figures whether or not he or she likes them. If adults don't like one of the authority figures in their lives, they can cast an opposing vote, find a new job, or move to a different community. In the meantime, while they are free to disagree with that authority figure, they are not free to disobey. It is my old-fashioned feeling that we adults have a responsibility to prepare children so they are capable of making a successful adjustment to the real world.

I think you ought to tell the teacher what I once told one of my daughter's high school teachers: "I don't agree with how you handle some situations, but I'm here to say I will support your decisions, whether I agree with them or not. Moreover, I will insist that Amy obey you, and there will be consequences if she doesn't." That was in Amy's best long-term interests, and it will be for your son as well.

In the meantime, I suspect you should put some effort into your son's discipline at home. In all likelihood, what you're describing is not so much a child who has some innate aversion to demanding adults as a child who simply hasn't learned to do what adults tell him to do.

6
Final Exam

You have just completed Family Building 101: Back to the Basics. As your professor, I sincerely hope that taking the course has been stimulating, eye-opening, and life-changing for you. But reading isn't enough. An academic course of study usually culminates in a final exam, and Family Building 101 is no exception. The exam consists of ten true or false questions per chapter, or fifty in all, the answers to which can be found following the exam, but no peeking! The test is not timed, but if you have actually read the whole book, you should be finished within eight hours. No bathroom breaks are allowed, and just in case someone—there's one in every crowd—has written certain essential information on his or her arm, no one will be allowed to wear long sleeves. Are you ready? Then please begin.

Chapter One

1. In a family, the husband-wife relationship should be no stronger than the relationship between the parents and the children; otherwise the children will be terribly insecure.

2. Parents bringing children into stepfamilies and blended families need to reassure their children, before the new marriage takes place, that the stepparent will not be allowed to discipline them.

3. In a family where the parent-child relationship is dominant, the child in question may have difficulty emancipating when the time comes.

4. An eight-year-old who is on a championship soccer team today will probably still be playing soccer when he or she is thirty years old.

5. A good number of discipline problems could be solved by simply reducing the level of stress in the family.

6. One easy way of reducing a family's level of stress is to enroll children in as many extracurricular activities as possible and attend every one of their sessions or games.

7. Most studies have found that children who spend significant time in day-care centers are more peaceful when resolving disputes than children who do not attend day care.

8. Many of today's moms are trying to clear the mother bar, which consists of messages to the effect that the busiest mother is the best mother.

9. The new ideal in American fatherhood is being your child's best buddy.

10. The family bed, where everyone sleeps together, is a wonderfully cozy idea that clearly lets the children know they are not members of the wedding.

Chapter Two

11. Effective discipline is mostly a matter of mastering various methods, such as time-out, taking away of privileges, star charts, and the like.

12. The most important of the "Three C's of Effective Discipline" is the use of proper *consequences.*

13. In essence, discipline is the process by which parents turn a child into a disciple, someone who will follow their lead.

14. Alpha Speech is the sort of talk one hears in a fraternity house after midnight on Saturday night.

15. It is possible for a parent, using proper disciplinary techniques, to control a child's behavior.

16. The notion that one can prevent behavior problems by simply giving instructions authoritatively is absurd.

17. Allowing a child to control the parent-child relationship causes the child to develop high self-esteem and more respect for the parent.

18. Sending a child to bed early might cause the child to develop negative feelings about his bed and his bedroom or even begin having nightmares.

19. Consequences, in order to be meaningful, need to be memorable.

20. Being consistent confirms your commitment to helping the child learn to control his or her behavior.

Chapter Three

21. High self-esteem is associated with higher achievement in school.

22. In the 1960s and early 1970s, America adopted new and better child-rearing principles and methods.

23. When driving, you would rather cut off a person with low self-esteem than a person with high self-esteem.

24. Self-respect and self-esteem mean pretty much the same thing.

25. Toddlers throw tantrums when they don't get their way because they have low self-esteem.

26. People with high self-esteem tend to feel a strong sense of obligation to others.

27. Self-respect is developed by giving respect away to other people.

28. We call a child who is suffering from low self-esteem a "spoiled brat."

29. Children's birthday parties should be modest, family-only affairs.

30. Children need a certain amount of praise but not a lot.

Chapter Four

31. People with good character always have good manners.

32. Today's parents tend to say one thing and do another: for example, they say manners are more important than grades, but they spend more

time helping their children get good grades than they do helping them develop good manners.

33. Good manners are a way of showing respect for others.

34. You should teach a child that if he wants to interrupt an adult conversation, he should say "excuse me."

35. Today's parents tend to spend a lot of time on matters that are of little ultimate importance, and little time on matters that are of great ultimate importance.

36. If you nag about it enough, a child will eventually learn good manners.

37. Good manners come naturally to a child.

38. Children raised in homes where religious values are stressed are less likely to use drugs and engage in premarital sex than children raised in homes where religious values are not stressed.

39. One good thing is that today's children cheat on tests less than did children forty or fifty years ago.

40. If you make a project of teaching a certain manner, it should be learned within a week or two.

Chapter Five

41. Responsibility consists of a good work ethic and a willingness to be fully accountable when it comes to one's own behavior.

42. Parents should pay children for doing chores around the house.

43. If it's a choice between chores and extracurricular activities, the latter should win out because they are going to benefit a child more in the long run.

44. Chores help children develop essential citizenship skills.

45. Today's parents all seem to think their children are gifted, but they tend to treat them like idiots.

46. A child who says he or she hasn't been treated fairly really means "I didn't get my way."

47. Today's children, partly because they lack chores or other means of forming a sense of obligation to their families, are growing up with a sense of entitlement that is eventually going to weaken American culture and the economy.

48. If your child feels that a teacher has given him or her a lower grade than he or she deserves, you should be your child's advocate.

49. A significant number of today's parents feel it is their responsibility to protect their children from negative consequences.

50. Since parents began helping children with their homework, national achievement test scores have been going downhill.

Answers to Family Building 101 Final Exam

1. F	11. F	21. F	31. T	41. T
2. F	12. F	22. F	32. T	42. F
3. T	13. T	23. T	33. T	43. F
4. F	14. F	24. F	34. F	44. T
5. T	15. F	25. F	35. T	45. T
6. F	16. F	26. F	36. F	46. T
7. F	17. F	27. T	37. F	47. T
8. T	18. F	28. F	38. T	48. F
9. T	19. T	29. T	39. F	49. T
10. F	20. T	30. T	40. T	50. T

It's completely up to you to decide what your score means. In any case, a parent who scores below 40 is probably in dire need of a good kick in the seat of the pants.

References and Suggested Readings

Baumeister, Roy F., et al. "Relation of Threatened Egotism to Violence and Aggression: The Dark Side of High Self-Esteem." *Psychological Review* 103, no. 1 (1996): 5–33.

Baumrind, Diana. "The Development of Instrumental Competence Through Socialization." Minnesota Symposium on Child Psychology, vol. 7, no. 35, 1993.

"Bullies Shove Their Way into the Nation's Schools." *USA Today,* September 7, 1999, Life section, 1.

Czudner, Gad. *Small Criminals Among Us—How to Recognize and Change Children's Antisocial Behavior Before They Explode.* Far Hills, N.J.: New Horizon Press, 1999.

Healy, Jane. *Endangered Minds: Why Our Children Don't Think and What to Do About It.* New York: Simon and Schuster, 1991.

Hymowitz, Kay. *Ready or Not: Why Treating Children as Small Adults Endangers Their Future—And Ours.* New York: Free Press, 1999.

Kellerman, Jonathan. *Savage Spawn.* New York: Ballantine Books, 1999.

Newberger, Eli H. *The Men They Will Become.* Reading, Mass.: Perseus Books, 1999.

Pollack, William. *Real Boys: Rescuing Our Sons from the Myths of Boyhood.* New York: Owl Books, 1999.

Samenow, Samuel. *Before It's Too Late—Why Some Kids Get into Trouble and What Parents Can Do About It.* New York: Times Books, 1998.

Whitehead, Barbara Dafoe, and David Popenoe. "Defining Daddy Down." *The American Enterprise,* September–October 1999, 31–34.

Yeoman, Barry. "Bad Girls." *Psychology Today,* November–December 1999, 54–57, 71.

About John Rosemond

John is a family psychologist, the author of ten best-selling parenting books, a syndicated columnist whose weekly parenting column runs in more than two hundred newspapers, and one of America's busiest and most popular public speakers. In a typical year, John delivers more than two hundred presentations and workshops to audiences of parents, teachers, businesspeople, physicians, and other professionals.

John's *real* qualifications, however, are that he and Willie have been married for thirty-seven years; they have two children, Eric and Amy, both of whom are married and doing well in all respects; and they are grandparents to six children, ranging in age from two to ten. John and Willie live in Gastonia, North Carolina.

John is executive director of the Center for Traditional Parenting in Gastonia, which provides resources for parents who want to raise their children in accord with traditional precepts. The center also publishes a quarterly magazine, *Traditional Parent,* which is read by more than ten thousand subscribers around the country.

To obtain information on John's books and audio materials (both CD and DVD) and *Traditional Parent* magazine, to read his weekly column, and to access his speaking schedule, go to John's web site, www.rosemond.com. For information on securing John as a public speaker, e-mail Willie Rosemond at whrosemond@aol.com. For information on John's Scripture-based parenting program, "Parenting by the Book," go to www.parentingbythebook.com.